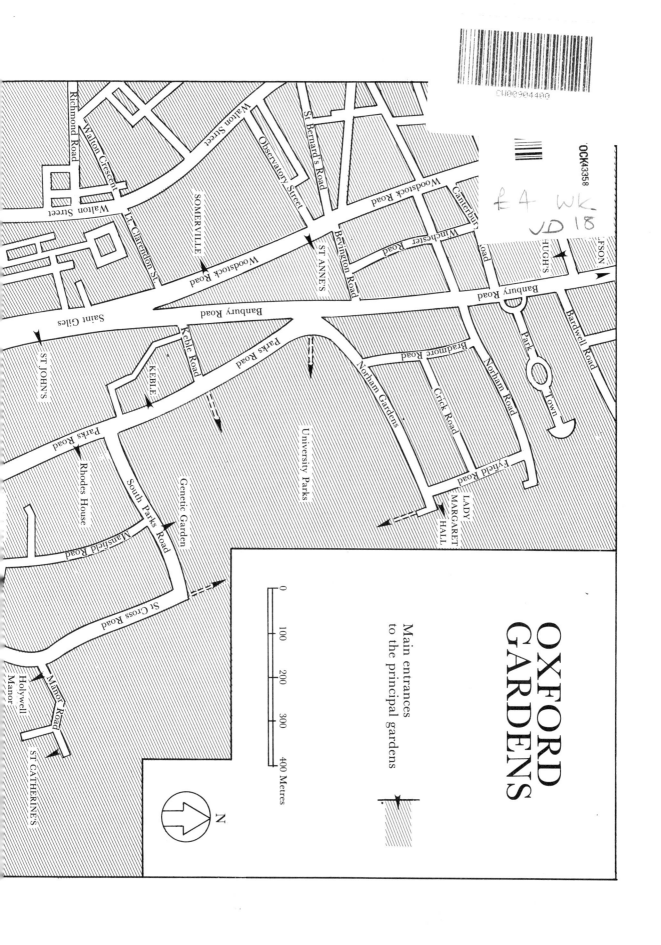

OXFORD GARDENS

Main entrances
to the principal gardens

0 100 200 300 400 Metres

N

OCK43358

£4 wk.
√D 18

OXFORD GARDENS

Text by
RONALD GRAY

With photographs by
ERNEST FRANKL

THE PEVENSEY PRESS
Cambridge England

Front cover Wadham's Back Quad: in the distance a superb silver lime; in the foreground, a Tree of Heaven, with its reddish winged seeds.

Back cover The Peruvian lily, *Alstroemeria*, in the Bog Garden at the far end of the Botanic Garden.

Published by The Pevensey Press
6 De Freville Avenue, Cambridge CB4 1HR, UK

Photographs: Ernest Frankl, except 6, 8, 10, 12, 18: Ronald Gray

Map: Carmen Frankl

Advice and help is gratefully acknowledged from: Dr I.J.R. Aitchison, Professor John L. Barton, Mavis Batey, Dr Angus Bowie, T.F.R.G. Braun, J.K. Burras, John Brooke, John Buxton, Dr F.A.L. Clowes, Dame Sylvia Crowe, Dr Jonathan Cohen, the Domestic Bursars of Exeter and Magdalen Colleges, Dr R.A. Dwek, Dr John Iles, John Kaye, Dr Barbara Levick, Dr R.L. Lucas, Dr D.J. Mabberley, John R.L. Maddicott, Professor Kathleen Major, Dr Alan Milner, A.M. Moodie, Dr D.E. Olleson, Dr Donald Pigott, Harry G. Pitt, John M. Prest, Alan Quarterman, Margaret E. Rayner, Dr David Stirzaker, Susan Strange, Dr Marjorie Sweeting, Marion Taylor, Rachel E. Trickett and Dr E.A.O. Whiteman

Edited by T.V. Buttrey

Designed by Jim Reader
Design and production in association with
Book Production Consultants, Cambridge

ISBN 0 907115 27 6

Typesetting in Baskerville by Ann Buchan Typesetters), Shepperton, Middlesex

Printed by Hazell, Watson & Viney, Aylesbury, England

Contents

A Tour of Oxford Gardens

The Medieval Centre

The gardens of colleges in italic type are described individually in the second part of the book.

College gardens vary greatly in scope and size. They also vary in times of opening, so that a tour including more than a few at a time is impracticable. The following account explains some of the variations, and groups the gardens by areas, so that plans for visiting any one group can be more easily made. For the sake of clarity, each area is explored by a route that can be followed from the map provided on the endpapers.

Looking from *Christ Church* Meadow at the great line of cathedral spire, towers, bastions and battlemented walls, you are seeing the broad end of a stretch of land, itself quite narrow, that thrusts south between the wide water-meadows of the Thames or Isis to the west, and of the Cherwell to the east. Surprisingly the Romans never used this natural fortress with its river-moats, though Anglo-Saxon settlements were scattered along its whole length, especially on the gravel patches (over Oxford clay) and the gravel terrace stretching from what is now the centre along St Giles and Banbury Road. But the Normans saw the advantages and built their castle mound, still standing near the river at the western extremity of the medieval city. The line of the city wall, surrounding the medieval precincts, begins behind the castle mound in Paradise Street, named after the 'Paradise' or garden of the Grey Friars, which used to lie just outside the wall. Passing north of the car-park you come to Pembroke, where the wall still runs along the southern front in Brewer Street, and where in 1675 the gardens included a small mound, a bowling green, a floral clock, arbours, and parallel beds of flowers or vegetables, though nothing of these remains.

Crossing St Aldate's, the wall ran along the south of *Christ Church* and the cathedral, and thence straight from west to east along the southern fronts of Corpus Christi and *Merton* Colleges, with many benefits to their gardens. Corpus derives great advantages from the wall, though its gardens are small: to enjoy the prospect here you should, ideally, climb the long steps from the lower ramparts to the high terrace at dawn with a companion after a Commem. Ball and see the sunlight flood in from one side over the plain. Merton, like all medieval colleges, once preferred kitchen produce; today, the walks along the walls look down on lawns, groves, and a rock-garden.

The wall turns north at the corner of Merton till it reaches after a gap St Edmund Hall and *New College* (**2**), whose garden is enhanced by the tall battlements bordering it. Turning another corner and running westward, the wall peters out not far from Catte Street, but its line is still indicated by Ship Street, roughly parallel with the northern side of Broad Street, where there was once a

1 *Worcester's lake was reclaimed from swamp in the early 19th century. From here, beneath the chestnuts, the college buildings are hidden by the arboretum.*

5

market-place outside the gates. It continued after that more or less straight alongside St Michael's Street through what is now St Peter's, whose premises provide no room for a garden, back to the castle mound.

By the end of the Middle Ages most of the colleges clustering round the centre had used up what little space they had. Oriel once had a garden of some size, in the area of the present Middle Quadrangle. Neglected before the Reformation, for two centuries after that it flourished. In the 18th century the great naturalist Gilbert White was a Fellow. But today only a few trees and small beds remain, though the 17th-century gates are delicately carved with roses, thistles, oak and vine leaves.

University College had in 1675 some small gardens with floral knots, topiary, a dovecote and a lean-to arbour. The existing Master's Garden and Fellows' Garden are both closed to the public, but a great variety of climbing plants decorate its quadrangles. The college has also transformed the eastern part of its precincts with the help of Dame Sylvia Crowe, who developed Logic Lane into a coherent whole and devised the very pleasing Cicely Court, an intimate corner planned in memory of a Master's wife.

Across the High towards its eastern end lies another group of colleges within the old city boundary, with an intricate net of quadrangles. St Edmund Hall is remembered by visitors as much for its great wisterias (**4**) as for its gables and informal quad, which is unusual in having a medieval well, discovered in 1927. The new well-head has a Latin quotation from Isaiah XII.3, translated in the Authorised Version as 'Therefore with joy shall ye draw water out of the wells of salvation.' St Edmund of Abingdon is said to have spoken this passage on his death-bed; if the saint did in fact live in a house on the site of the Hall he would have used this well. The garden of the college is the former churchyard of St Peter's in the East, with many ancient yews and tombstones; the church itself is now the college library. Mathematicians may understand the inscription on a seat in the churchyard, AM. $e^2/\hbar$c. DG, giving praise to God for a discovery in quantum mechanics. The city wall divides this part from New College.

Queen's has made so much use of the little space available as to need a separate account. All Souls, on the other hand, and Hertford, next door to the north, have nothing by way of garden to show the public. On the other side of Radcliffe Camera, Brasenose no longer has the knot gardens that in the 17th century occupied what is now Old Quad, but the charming Chapel Quad to the left still preserves a herbaceous border with flowering trees. (Not far away, however, Brasenose has a hostel, Frewin Hall, opposite St Peter's College, that is well worth a visit for its ingenious use of former back gardens.) Just across Brasenose Lane, is *Exeter College*, with a garden of great intimate charm. Lincoln, adjoining, has gardens for its Rector and Fellows, but these are closed to the public. A small quad, still called the Grove, has one great London plane; the vines in Chapel Quad, not the ones originally planted, preserve a tradition of vine-growing here four hundred years old. Front Quad is enhanced in autumn by a brilliant red Virginia creeper (**3**).

As you step out of Exeter or Lincoln into Turl Street, the grand old spherical horse chestnut overhanging the road is a fine sight. It belongs to Jesus College, which has good wisterias but is particularly memorable for its very high wall along Ship Street, topped with wallflowers, valerian, and the yellow Oxford ragwort that has spread down railway embankments across the entire countryside.

The only other college within, or rather partly within, the medieval precincts is Nuffield, laid out in accordance with the wishes of Lord Nuffield in the traditional style of Oxford colleges, but with a garden more French in its symmetry. The long rectangular pool with water-lilies and irises, steps rising to a square fountain flanked by four rectangular rose-beds, all suggest a nave and chancel. In the corner

the spired tower in fact houses the library. (The fountain is the work of Hubert Dalwood, a pupil of Henry Moore; the sculpture on the wall, *Apparition*, is by F.I. Kormis.) The best view is from Worcester Street, through the western arch, especially when the climbing roses facing the pool are in bloom.

North and West of the Centre

Some of the best of Oxford's gardens lie outside the medieval city. *Worcester's* spacious lake and arboretum (**1**) are north of the castle. *Balliol's* garden is comparatively small, though well maintained, and much used. *Wadham*, close to the ancient city wall, has a famous garden with a long history, and Rhodes House, just north of Wadham, has one of the most colourful herbaceous borders, as well as fine trees. Manchester and Mansfield, backing on to Wadham, have only private gardens for their Principals. But *Trinity* and *St John's*, dividing between them the Benedictine lands north of Broad Street, have vast sweeps of lawn, and freedom to experiment with groves and terraces, long herbaceous borders, sunken gardens.

One striking feature of these extramural colleges is their variety of levels. Earthworks thrown up in the Civil War, as at Wadham and *St Catherine's*, still provide slopes and high walks, while former quarries, left unfilled, make possible steep descents into rose gardens, as at *Keble*. Old gravel quarries since built over make half the charm of St Anne's, where a row of terrace houses in Bevington Road with their steep-ended gardens has been taken over en bloc, providing a vista of domestic peace from behind Hartland House. A good many of St Anne's gardens are still those of former private houses, including the garden provided for a crèche.

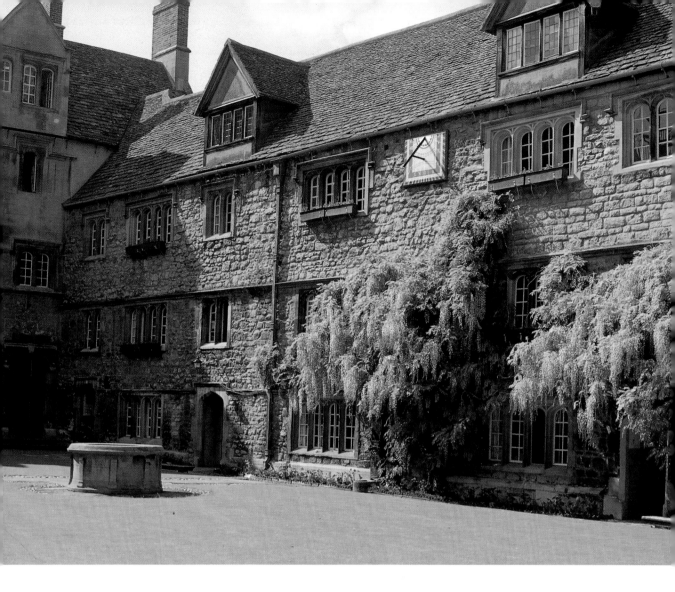

But the central area between Wolfson and Rayne Buildings and the dining hall is an innovation, half glade, half quad, where a cedar, a cypress, a catalpa, an oak, a copper beech and other trees rise over a wide area. A plan for a lake on the Banbury Road side was never realised. *Somerville*, not far from the Woodstock Road and Banbury Road fork, and nearer the city centre than St Anne's, has more space than most colleges, on this side of the city, but has not made gardens so much as planted trees and climbing plants. Green College, just north of Somerville, has taken over the superb 18th-century Radcliffe Observatory, whose high octagonal tower now overlooks a small (private) landscaped area.

St Antony's, further north beyond St Anne's, has pleasant greenswards and old trees but is too recent a foundation to have developed its gardens notably. *St Hugh's*, however, the most northerly college along Banbury Road, has occupied many acres with a Victorian dell, a nut-walk, shrubberies, orchards, greenhouses and avenues, as well as a terraced garden unrivalled anywhere in the University. These are gardens well off the beaten track for tourists, and not to be missed.

North and East of the Centre

To see a most distinctive array of separate gardens you need to move eastwards from St Hugh's to visit, first, *Wolfson*, preferably taking in Park Town (1853-5), a Victorian railed-in oval bounded by two crescent roads, privately owned but open to visitors. From Wolfson, for a mile and a half down to Christ Church Meadow, the Cherwell flows between willows and alders, past Dragon School and Parson's Pleasure, Dames' Delight and Mesopotamia. In a punt you are scarcely aware of anything but leafy vistas, birds, bathers, and the occasional other boat. Turn off the river at Wolfson, however, and you are in a man-made harbour, with a sloping natural garden rising to some of the most varied and specialised plantings of recent years. Alternatively, the path along the eastern bank (entered from either the college or Marston Ferry Road) will take you as far as the high arched bridge leading into *University Parks* (see p.12), where the walk continues on the western bank until you are opposite *Magdalen* Fellows' Garden (and here you have no choice but to turn back). But these are nature rambles: to see the gardens you need to make repeated sallies from the roads parallel to the river. *Lady Margaret Hall* displays formal beds of extraordinary beauty, gradually giving way to riverside walks. Linacre, at the south entrance to University Parks, has steps down to a courtyard garden, and a pleasant domestic garden at the rear, with lawn and woodland corner, once part of a nunnery. Further south lies St Catherine's, whose gardens have the distinction of being planned throughout by the architect of its buildings, presenting completely new conceptions of college gardening.

Here, however, the river can no longer be followed by boat or on foot. To reach Magdalen, leave St Catherine's by the main entrance, follow round Manor Road and Longwall Street and turn left at the High. On your right, across the road, lies Magdalen's Penicillin Garden (**5**), given by Albert and Mary Lasker to commemorate the medical development by Florey, Chain and others of Sir Alexander Fleming's original discovery. Designed by Dame Sylvia Crowe, it met strong opposition from those who held it would contradict the character of already

5 *Designed by Dame Sylvia Crowe, the rose garden near the entrance to the Botanic Garden commemorates the Oxford scientists who developed the medical applications of penicillin.*

6 *The 'rainbow' bridge, built in 1923–4 to help relieve mass unemployment, gracefully spans the Cherwell in University Parks.*

existing, informally grouped trees, though a formal garden had already existed there at one time, and the area had now become in her view 'ragged and nondescript'. As Dame Sylvia wrote to the author, her concern was to 'preserve the scale and dignity of the High, and to give an appropriate approach to the Botanic Garden'. To achieve this she 'planted the strong feature of a yew hedge and buttresses to give a dignified frontage, in scale with the High, and contained the rose-beds in box hedges to give solidity to the design and a fitting foreground to the distinguished building at the end', while leaving the detail of each bed to be enjoyed within the walks. She planted pleached copper beech at the west end to accentuate the architectural framework, while the whitebeam in the corner matches those at Magdalen across the road. There can be few small gardens with so many thousands of blooms in show at one time.

The *Botanic Garden* (see p. 69), and Magdalen opposite, contribute two more riverside gardens, the one on this side dominated by its good greenhouses, the other almost natural, like the very large wooded island, *Angel and Greyhound Meadow* (the strange name derives from two pubs), stretching north from Magdalen Bridge. As you cross the bridge you look down on to the private Magdalen College School grounds, white bridges gleaming against the foliage. Still further on, a garden, often unnoticed, occupies the centre of The Plain, a traffic roundabout. Turning right into Cowley Place you reach *St Hilda's*, where the riverside site is turned to splendid advantage.

To survey all Oxford at once, continue from The Plain up St Clement's Street towards Headington. Headington Hill Park has good trees. South Park, on the other side of Headington Road, is also well provided, and from the top of the slope you are able to survey the whole city of Matthew Arnold's dreaming spires.

University Parks

The vast open space here has been used by students drilling to oppose the landing of the Duke of Monmouth or to fight the Boers, by Charles II to walk his dog, for Coronation tea parties, and is still used for cricket matches against Commonwealth and county teams. At the same time it is in effect a huge arboretum. The guide to its trees (1976), obtainable from booksellers, or from the Superintendent at South Lodge, lists over eight hundred, perhaps as many shrubs, all pinpointed on large-scale maps. There have been many changes, owing to the freak storm of 2–3 January 1976, the severe gale of 24 March 1986, the deaths of many elms, and the great number of recent plantings.

For points of reference there are the big, unmistakable *Sophora japonica* just left of the Keble Gate, and the ten cherries planted down the path to the right, including 'Shimidsu Sakura', 'Sargentii', 'Kanzan' and 'Okame'. Alternatively, entering by the North Lodge gate and walking east, there are trees enough to raise spirits even on a dull day: a Tree of Heaven within a hundred yards eastwards, a horse chestnut with circular seat, beyond which (some 25 paces) is a 'Gutta Percha' Tree, recognisable by the latex strands showing in a torn leaf, then a beech drooping hugely across the path, and a great group of cedars facing the cricket pavilion. This path will lead you eastwards past the end of a long avenue of varied hawthorns on your right, towards the large lily pond (after a left-hand fork) created in 1926. From the pond the high 'rainbow' bridge (**6**), built in 1923-4 as a project to relieve mass unemployment, can be easily reached, and a solitary walk further southward to Music Meadow and Great Meadow, with the prospect of a romantic pool and three islands near Magdalen Walks, is inviting.

Only the official guide can really cope with the trees. But if *Taxus baccata* 'Dovastoniana' or *Sorbus torminalis*, both fairly rare in this country, interest you, or the *Salix alba* planted in 1967 to commemorate the record score of 192 not out made by R. Kanhai for the West Indies against the University, the guide is what you need.

Oxford City and Environs

The City Council's gardens and parks mostly lie a good distance from the centre. In addition to the superb South Park and Headington Hill Park, Cutteslowe Park, north of the ring road, is well known for its flower gardens and ornamental wildfowl, while Bury Knowle Park, beyond the brow of Headington Hill beside the London road, has fine trees.

Only one domestic garden within the city boundary is named in the annual list of gardens open on certain days under the National Gardens Scheme (by post from 57 Lower Belgrave St., London SW1W OLR), but many more are only a few miles away. At Boars Hill to the south is Jarns Mound, created as a wild garden by the archaeologist Sir Arthur Evans. Landscaped gardens on the grand scale, Blenheim, Ditchley, Rousham and others, are described by Mavis Batey in *Of Oxfordshire Gardens*, Oxford Polytechnic Press 1982.

7 *Addison's Walk, Magdalen.*

The Colleges

Balliol College

Like some of the newest colleges in Oxford, Balliol began by acquiring small houses and absorbing their back yards into one whole. That was in the 13th century, however, and the gardens today are a creation of the mid-19th, though the lawn in Front Quad owes its pleasing 18th-century ellipse to a restoration of the 1950s. Notable in this quad are the wisteria and wallflowers, the *Trochodendron* whose flowers are like spokes of a wheel, a *Colletia cruciata* with flat triangular spines (opposite the entrance gate) and a *Poncirus trifoliata*, with spiny branches bearing a strange fruit, half orange, half lemon.

As you emerge from Front Quad, passing the *Poncirus* on your left, into Garden Quad (**9**), two horse chestnuts, a silver birch and a copper beech dominate the scene, with a herbaceous border to the east, supplemented by abutilons and roses (*R. chinensis mutabilis* and *R. Highdownensis*) twice a year. Rose-beds lie in front of the buildings facing you, and in spring a magnolia's white blossoms enhance the triangular porch and steps of the dining hall, the best features of Waterhouse's design. The garden is constantly used by people reading, sitting around or playing croquet and bowls throughout the summer afternoons. Even at night, after club dinners, there takes place the ritual singing of the 'Gordouli', an awe-inspiring denunciation originally meant for an innocent and long-since dead undergraduate of the adjoining college, Trinity, now hurled at its every single member, as unsuspecting guests at the Randolph Hotel have been horrified to hear.

Further to the right is the private but easily seen Fellows' Garden with the so-called Tomb of Devorguilla (wife of the founder John Balliol; **8**), built of stones from the college's old entrance, demolished in the late 1860s. The two mulberries were planted in 1857 when Butterfield designed the chapel and the Fellows' Garden. An older specimen, just outside the wall and close to the catalpa, is possibly one of the famous James I mulberries, planted about 1608 in the hope of creating an industry based on silkworms.

Holywell Manor, the Balliol hostel for graduate students about ten minutes walk away in Manor Road, honours the diarist John Evelyn (1620–1706), a college member famous for gardening. Some remnants of the building date from the early 16th century. It was extended in the 1930s by the architects Kennedy and Nightingale, to whom the basic layout of the garden is due: a long rectangular sunken lawn between two low L-shaped walls, the ends turning away from each other at right angles to provide a vista from the house down an avenue of ginkgos and rose bushes towards two cherries which form a haze of blossom in spring. With a dark and huge horse chestnut at the far end, this might have been created as a stage for the Balliol Players, whose performances here were famous for years. The 'foyer' of the theatre, nearest the house, has a pool and fountain, where there is a

8 The 'Tomb of Devorguilla', in the Fellows' Garden of Balliol, celebrates the wife of John Balliol, founder of the college in the mid-13th century.

sculpture by Peter Lyon (very like his sculpture at Park Town private garden). The gradation from this formality to the 'natural' garden at the far end is beautifully achieved, and the whole deserves a visit from all who care about Oxford gardens.

Christ Church and the Meadow

The parts of the college usually on view are, with two exceptions, treated formally. Four lawns surround the lily pool in Tom Quad with its fountain and copy of Giovanni da Bologna's *Mercury*. Peckwater Quad (**10**) has had since 1978 an interesting formal Baroque layout of lawns based on an unexecuted design shown in Williams's print of 1732. The famous trees, however, a fig and an oriental plane, though probably the largest of their kind in the country, cannot be seen from any part to which the public is admitted. Both were brought back from the East by Edward Pococke in 1636. There is just a glimpse of the huge branches of the plane from the Meadow Walk leading up to Merton.

In the cathedral (the college chapel), the tomb of Lady Montacute (died 1354) bears what is perhaps the first recorded columbine, common in the Meadow. The earliest record of the sycamore in England is allegedly the one to be seen in a carving of leaves and winged seeds on the reconstructed tomb of St Frideswide (probably 1289; left of the high altar). A garden with many medieval features, designed in 1985 by Mavis Batey, lies in the former cloister garth on the south side of the cathedral. The raised beds, trellis railing and earthenware pots, and a flowery mead such as Chaucer describes in *The Franklin's Tale*, are not a restoration or reproduction, but an associative garden with features taken from medieval

9 *Balliol's Garden Quad, in the early morning of May Day, a time of general celebrations.*

10 *The lawns of Peckwater Quad, Christ Church, shaped in 1978, follow the pattern suggested in an illustration of the college dated 1732.*

illustrations. They include those seen in the borders of the illuminated lectionary Cardinal Wolsey gave his college in 1528: Tudor roses, madonna lilies, flax, heartsease, carnations, wild strawberries, violets, irises and borage. Catherine of Aragon's pilgrimage to St Frideswide's shrine in 1518, when she was accompanied by Wolsey, is commemorated by a pomegranate tree, the pomegranate being the symbol of Granada, conquered by her parents Ferdinand and Isabella.

East of the cathedral the broad lawn and herbaceous borders of the 'Master's Garden' (**12**) can be glimpsed through the gates on Christ Church Meadow.

By contrast the War Memorial Garden (**11**) is wide open to the public, and is in spirit as much a memorial to men of Oxford City as to members of the college. Designed by John Coleridge in 1925–6, it makes good dramatic use of the sloping part of the site. You enter through iron gates by R.M.Y. Gleadowe, walking over an inscription taken from Bunyan's Mr Valiant-for-Truth: 'My sword I give to him that shall succeed me in my pilgrimage', and with that the garden takes on a new aspect.

To your left is a long low terrace, planted with lupins, delphiniums, rock roses, climbing roses, poppies and lavatera. A round projection resembles a bastion, while rising above at some distance up the hill is the tall-windowed dining hall, battlemented and looking half like a castle, so that there is a suggestion of spiritual warfare suiting the theme Bunyan's words imply. To your right, the lawn is bare of flowers, but as you cross the bridge over Trill Mill stream (a millwheel lies beyond) a circular garden appears: in the centre the Serpent Fountain that stood in Tom Quad from 1670 to 1695, and surrounding this, first a wide circular band of lemon-yellow Lady's Mantle, or alchemilla, then an equally wide one of rugosa

roses, all against a background of curving red-brick wall. In June madonna lilies raise their heads higher than the wall lining the bridge.

This is the grand entrance to the open spaces of Christ Church Meadow. Until the mid-1970s there was a view straight down Broad Walk towards the distant avenue of elms, planted in the 1680s by Dr Fell, which seemed to Robert Southey like the original source of Gothic naves; all dead now, of course. Taking their place are planes: it was at one time discussed whether to plant both occidental and oriental planes, together with the hybrid London plane propagated in the Botanic Garden in the 1660s. But the occidental plane does not thrive here as the others do, and these alone are planted, parent and offspring alternately, along the length of the Walk, some three hundred yards.

In fifty years the new avenue will be majestic. At present it is better to turn half right, away from the bare path, down Poplar Walk or New Walk, originally planted in 1872. On your right, hundreds of rabbits scutter in the bushes, quite bold. On your left, cattle graze in the great expanse of water-meadow, Magdalen's beautiful tower in the distance. At the end of the Walk come racing eights on the Thames or Isis, sea-going pleasure launches, steamers, dinghies with outboard motors. This riverside path, once known as the Dean's Ham, stretches down to the bridge over the Cherwell. Figwort, dock, silverweed, comfrey grow along the bank, while across the bridge lie the liners' foc's'les of the new college boathouses. But turn left here, where the Cherwell joins the Isis, and the best part of the Meadow begins.

Joseph Addison must have found this path every bit as agreeable as Magdalen Walks, though there is less of art mixed with nature here. Some of the unusual trees planted in 1954 may still be found: *Acer macrophyllum*, *A. spicatum*, *A. crataegifolium*. Spindle Trees and new alders also stand along the banks. Thousands of daffodils

11 *Rising banks of catmint, lupins and lavatera lead the eye from Christ Church War Memorial Garden to the college's gothic dining hall.*

12 *Looking across the 'Master's Garden' of Christ Church to the medieval city wall alongside the garden of Corpus Christi, with the tower of Merton chapel beyond.*

18

were planted in the early 1960s by the Friends of the Meadow. But the wild tulip has been there a long time, and the columbine is common. The most interesting and strangely impressive tree in Oxford is the *Zelkova carpinifolia* that stands a few hundred yards from the Cherwell–Isis confluence. Easily recognisable by its great fan of thick branches spraying out like a broom from twenty feet up, it comes from the Caucasus, and is a relative of the English elm that has not suffered from the recent Black Death. Its girth in 1912, measured round what seem like a dozen trunks in one, was 12 feet 8 inches (386cm). The mighty oriental planes and London planes nearby are less mysterious, but shade over the *Zelkova*, so that you see it like a shrine at the end of a green vista. Another of the same species, further along near the ferry, does not have the same effect. But there is something imposing about many of these trees along the Cherwell: the poplar that leans over at 45°, the chestnut at the far end, towering near the avenue of pollarded limes leading to Rose Lane and the Botanic Garden – few rivers in England have such giants along their banks.

Across the Meadow is one of the great views of Oxford, the long line of Tom Tower, cathedral spire, Merton's square tower, the dome of Radcliffe Camera, and the façades of Corpus and Merton Colleges, glimpsed between hawthorns. There is also the chance of seeing kingfishers, the lesser-spotted woodpecker, hawfinches, siskins, snipe, swallows, yellow wagtails. No wonder that for generations the Meadow has been a favourite walk. John Locke collected plants here, Gilbert White probably did too; Ruskin drew them, Gerard Manley Hopkins wrote about them; Newman and Ronald Knox took exercise here, reading their breviaries. George Whitfield the Methodist preacher prayed under one of the trees 'for near two hours, sometimes lying flat on my face, sometimes kneeling upon my knees', while the stormy night 'gave me awful thoughts of the day of judgment'. Samuel Johnson as an undergraduate went sliding on the ice, and offered that as an excuse for not attending his tutorial.

These acres are full of associations. Along the path beneath Merton's walls runs Deadman's Walk, where until 1290, the year of their expulsion, Jews may have carried their dead from St Aldate's to their burial ground, now the Botanic Garden. In 1643 the Meadow was deliberately flooded for the defence of the city, and earthworks were built along and across the line of Broad Walk; vestiges of a bastion can still be seen. In the mid-19th century natural floods were deep enough for dinghies to sail over, and as recently as 1947 floods reached Broad Walk. By that time the elms, mostly planted in the 1660s, had begun to decay. Alice Liddell, daughter of the Dean of Christ Church, better known as Lewis Carroll's Alice in Wonderland, was one of those who planted a replacement in 1863. But hers has vanished with the rest.

Exeter College

In autumn Front Quad is bright red with Virginia creeper and in spring the magnolias blossom by the chapel. No college garden feels as domestic as Exeter Fellows' Garden (**13**), which is open from 2 to 4 p.m. almost every day. Where bigger colleges have regular parks, five or ten minutes' walk away, the Fellows' Common Room here looks straight on to the garden, and Fellows can sit outside on a warm day for coffee or claret as though at a private house.

There is no special rarity, but the L-shaped terrace overlooking Radcliffe Square, already constructed by 1650, gives a slight sense of drama, of being in some fortified place with battlements. Bishop Heber's chestnut at the corner is so big and old it is capable of bringing the whole wall down one day. An undergraduate superstition is that if its leaves touch the buildings of Brasenose, Exeter will bump Brasenose in the races on the river. The sloping quadrant beneath the terrace affords an amphitheatre for displaying the winter aconites, and anemones and daffodils all through the spring. The gardener's hut is artfully tucked away underneath the terrace, and the herbaceous border stretching back to the buildings is good, honest stuff, even though some dragon arums (*Dracunculus vulgaris*) lurk in it. One problem with the terrace quadrant is water supply. After spring and the tulips have gone, not much is left to nourish later plants. There is some hope of piping water from the pool, created in 1923 under the Bodleian windows – though the chestnuts will soak that up as they cover the area with still more shade. Yet the terrace is too good to lose.

Facing the herbaceous border is the library (1856-7), designed by Sir George Gilbert Scott, and now partly covered by wisteria and roses. Against the wall of the main building are four celebrated figs, recovering from recent hard winters and the cleaning of the stone. One at least of these was planted at the end of the 17th century, a cutting from a fig tree at Christ Church which came from the Holy Land. It is called Dr Kennicott's Fig after the distinguished 18th-century Hebrew scholar and Fellow of the college, who relished figs.

In Margary Quad, or Back Quad, the sculpture, by J. de Alberdi, is entitled *Logic and Imagination*.

13 *This corner of Exeter Fellows' Garden is bright with tulips and daffodils in spring.*

Keble College

Front Quad was provided with a sunken lawn to add even more height to Butterfield's Victorian chapel. But though typical of Oxford's varied levels, it is not a garden, and the main gardening interest is the Fellows' Garden beyond, through the entrance gates to the left of the chapel. In 1968 it was decided to illustrate Victorian ideas on design in the 1860s and 1870s, when the main part of the college was built; hence the beds of 'Victorian' begonias, pelargoniums and fuchsias at the northern end, in front of the pollarded limes. Ivy and holly, a weeping tree (here a False Acacia) and Michaelmas daisies are also typically Victorian, as are the collections of hostas beneath the limes and of ferns beneath the hornbeams, including *Dryopteris filix mas*, famous as a bottled fern needing practically no water or air. It is hoped to keep alive *Hesperis matronalis fl. pl. alba*, the old double sweet rocket, a favourite bedding plant in mid-Victorian days, and to bring in examples of Victorian garden furniture.

Moving south along the terrace between five large London planes into the area of the buildings of the mid-1970s is like moving into the Space Age. To see the large pebbled area surrounding ventilators and covering the flat roof of the Middle Common Room and college bar you really need to be inside the building, looking down. The almost complete absence of plants seems Zen in inspiration, and even the rose bushes at one side are small and scarcely visible from below. Two trees have been allowed by the architects to grow through openings, though their roots in a semi-basement feel no sun. At the far end a ten-year-old plane almost touches the closely encircling windows: it can only grow spindly, looking for light.

A pleasant (private) sunken and walled rose garden is just visible in the south-east corner, and a fine herbaceous border and copper beech in Pusey Quad.

Lady Margaret Hall

Spacious gardens of great variety, fields and riverside woods stretch round three sides. The way in is through the front (Wolfson) quad, past fine wisterias and *Clematis armandii*, and then after a turn to the right near the right-hand end, through the centenary gates of 1978. From here, however, the great expanse is still not really visible, though a pleasing formal garden with a sundial leads the eye to a blue Atlas cedar, planted in 1947, and opposite the gate a *Metasequoia* or dawn redwood that is not as yet doing very well.

Turn right again for the garden of Old Hall and the house which was the college's first home: it is still a domestic garden, with anemones, alchemilla, hosta, saxifrage, spirea, pokeweed and in the background yellow allium and a woodland area. *Tropaeolum speciosum* climbs over the bushes like shoals of red goldfish. A rockery here is being remodelled at the suggestion of the former Garden Steward, Dr Anne Whiteman, who over the years brought many plants for the college from the garden of John Aldridge, R.A., at Great Bardsfield, Essex.

On the short path behind Old Hall you pass a *Magnolia grandiflora* reaching to the eaves, and a tall herbaceous border with superb delphiniums, lupins, phlox, sunflowers. On your way back, at the corner of the building is that witch-like plant *Dracunculus vulgaris*, with spotted stem, a furled chocolate-coloured spathe, and later a spike like a cuckoopint. Here the gardens begin to open up. To the left, a splendid formal garden surrounding the bird-bath given by students who went down in 1925, against the background of a copper beech, planted about 1907. To the right, a punt dock, called 'the backwater', divides the gardens from the pond in

University Parks. Then on past the mixed field hedge and across the stream, a remnant of the old water-meadows, which has been encouraged to keep its rural beauty: fritillaries, cowslips and primroses have been planted here; as many as twenty snipe will nest by the hedge in a cold winter. Beyond the tennis courts perhaps the most rewarding part of the grounds begins. A leaflet to be had at the Porters' Lodge lists about 250 different wild plants growing in the whole area of the garden as well as 69 species of bird, and quantities of different dragonflies, grasshoppers, 20 butterflies, 183 moths, and 3 worms. (No match for the Revd Hilderic Friend who in 1904 and 1909 listed 17 of these in the Botanic Garden.) This is as delightful a piece of riverside (**15**) as any in Oxford. The rose walk planted in the 1950s does not obtrude on the rustic scene, nor does the circular bed of bluebells (later white irises) surrounding a small circular pool, overhung with a willow, known as the 'Eye of the Lord'. Something slightly suggesting ritual does appear here. The avenue of Lombardy poplars leading from the college buildings seems to be a path towards the dark pupil represented by the pool, its iris formed by the bluebells.

Further upstream, spring brings a grey-white mist of cow-parsley and tall silvery-grey willows. The path, passing through crowds of daffodils, was made in the 1940s. It leads on the right to a grassy sward, splendid with purple and white fritillaries (later martagon lilies). From the path there is a beautiful view up the willow-shaded Cherwell towards the Dragon School.

Turn left, however, before going so far, and you enter the Fellows' Garden, which has good roses but awaits remodelling. Over to the right, to one side of the summer-house, is a plaque commemorating H.C. Deneke, 'Garden Steward, L.M.H. 1925–1968', a great patron of music, of whom an endearing story is told: needing to ride a bicycle to survey her domains, a privilege not granted to anyone else, she meticulously and unfailingly gave hand-signals. The Woodland Garden at the rear is named after her, and the Caucasian wing nut is of her planting. She and Dr Elinor Gardner were mainly responsible for the layout of the college gardens as a whole.

The way back leads to the nearest (north-east) corner of the college past the end of the field-hedge – turn left before you come to the service area and pass through the herb garden. Fellows rather than college cooks use the borage, lovage, sage, angelica, sweet cicely, chives, rosemary and three kinds of mint.

Threading between the herbs and the fire tank, as you turn the corner of the building, the south range of Sir Giles Gilbert Scott's building comes into view, with cypresses and a terrace garden bright in spring with alyssum, rock roses, dianthus, campanula, linum, thyme and erigeron. Spleenwort fans out from wall crevices. A curiosity near the same corner is a holy thistle, *Silybum marianum*, raised here by the gardener Graham Ray after it planted itself by his kitchen door. (The odd name comes from the Greek *silubos*, a thistle.) Behind it is a honeysuckle in memory of 'Peg', a scout who was murdered.

You may wish to go back to the centenary gate, passing the neo-Wren building where there are more cypresses and a herbaceous border. Or retracing your steps you can visit the area outside the chapel, which has a pool with goldfish and golden orfe and has been landscaped in a slightly bumpy way. The climbing roses on the wall at the west end of Wolfson Quad are a triumph.

Magdalen College

Built outside the medieval city, Magdalen always had plenty of room for gardens and even for parks, which it has used to advantage. The first glimpse of the wealth here comes after you have passed the Porters' Lodge and the chapel and emerged from dark passages into the cloister, where in late May the long blossoms of seven wisterias stretch along the whole north wall. There are more wisterias beyond, on the classical façade of the New Building, and in St Swithun's Quad and Longwall Quad – not all of these are open to the public. Most notable is the 'Magdalen Plane', to your left as you face the New Building, planted in 1801, a scion of the hybrid (London) plane first raised in the Botanic Garden in 1666.

Until a few years ago, the even greater attraction was the Grove or Deer Park, still further to the left beyond the plane, but this has suffered irreparable loss from the disease which destroyed almost all the elms in England. The last batch were felled in 1978, when a ring-count showed the oldest to have been planted in 1689. (Oliver Wendell Holmes gave the girth of one in 1886 as 25 feet 6 inches (752cm); in 1899 it had reached 130 feet (3962cm) in height.) Before 1689, there had probably been neither elms nor deer. During the Civil War many trees were felled for fuel, and the University Regiment marched and countermarched across the open space. Trees planted soon after the end of that war were pulled down later, as having been planted by 'fanatics', presumably Puritans. But for nearly three hundred years the elms flourished, and the deer, introduced in about 1720, still do so, though they

16 *A* catalpa bignonioides *stands in front of Magdalen's New Building of 1733 (completed in 1824). To the right, almost hidden, is one of the college's many wisterias.*

now spend their summers in the water-meadows. Recent replantings of a great variety of trees – birch and gean near the walls, oak, hornbeam, lime in the centre, with manna ash, American oak and other rapid growers to protect the slower-growing native specimens – will ensure that no disease again denudes the whole area.

Retrace your steps eastward, past the New Building to the bridge over the Cherwell. Left and right are two of the finest herbaceous borders in Oxford, followed in late summer by a great array of dahlias. Crossing the bridge, you come to the Meadow, a part of the grounds for which Magdalen is still as famous as it is for its May-morning singing. Keep an eye open for swans and the great perch or pike that sun themselves, given a chance. Here begins the celebrated Addison's Walk (**7**, **18**), named after the Fellow of Magdalen whose influence on the evolution of English gardens was revolutionary. But all this, and more, would have been lost if Humphrey Repton's plan of 1801 for widening the Cherwell into a lake, flooding the Meadow, had been put into effect.

Addison, as a disciple of John Locke, the advocate of natural morality, was equally in favour of naturalness in gardens and landscaping. But just as Locke's morality required some civilised agreement, so Addison's 'natural scenes' were not meant to be nature untouched by art. 'We find the Works of Nature still more pleasing,' he wrote in *The Spectator* of 25 June 1712, 'the more they resemble those of Art: for in this case our Pleasure rises from a double Principle; from the Agreeableness of the Objects to the Eye, and from their Similitude to other Objects.' The Chinese, he adds, 'chuse rather to shew a Genius in Works of this Nature [i.e. gardens] and therefore always conceal the Art by which they direct themselves. They have a Word, it seems, in their language, by which they express the particular Beauty of a Plantation that thus strikes the Imagination at first Sight, without discovering [revealing] what it is that has so agreeable an Effect.'

Addison's Walk, although it has a natural appearance, is man-made. The causeway probably dates from the 16th century, and the trees are seldom the willows and alders that you find along the Cherwell in its upper reaches. In 1985, of some 350 trees along the Walks (the circuit was completed in the 19th century), over 100 were beeches, not suitable for sloping banks because of their shallow rooting systems; another 60 were horse chestnuts, 49 were yews, 34 English oaks and 30 hornbeams. Under the careful management of Dr Clowes a new balance is being struck. More alders will not only increase the naturalness but attract siskins and redpolls. Rowans will bring their brilliant red berries in August, and balsam poplars their scent. The self-sown sycamores and advancing snowberries will be drastically reduced, except where some scrub is needed to keep boating parties at a distance or to hold banks together. And perhaps the magnolias, of which there are a few, will yield place despite their beauty to plants that need no special efforts to keep them alive in these unfavourable soils. The problem of balancing nature and art continues to receive constant attention.

Less needs to be done to preserve spring flowers such as the buttercup called 'Goldilocks', often recognisable by its ragged petals, or 'Town Hall Clock' with its clusters of flowers, one pointing upwards and four facing outwards, or butcher's broom, or the summer-time leafless, brown *Monotropa hipopytis*, a total parasite that relies entirely on other plants for chlorophyll. It is a different story where the famous purple and white snake's-head fritillaries (**19**) are concerned. 'Scatter'd in myriads on the blushing ground', in the words of a poem by a demy, or scholar of Magdalen in the late 18th century, praised by Matthew Arnold in 'Thyrsis' (but at Eynsham and Sandford, just to the north and south), they were being picked in such numbers by 1908 that the President published a prohibition, to preserve them

17 *Looking past the end of Magdalen's New Building towards the Grove, where deer were kept as early as 1720.*

from extinction. They still need not only such a prohibition but also the most careful management. Until recently, the meadow was grazed by bullocks after the fritillaries had seeded, to allow the flowers a better chance of competing with the grasses. This resulted, however, in a predominance of buttercups, and it was decided to try transferring the fallow deer from the Grove for the summer months. So far the experiment has been successful: the fritillaries have begun to spread into the other half of the meadows, and there are hopes that in future the entire acreage will flourish in late April and May with these chequered lanterns on their curving necks.

The fritillaries are probably best seen from the eastern part of the Walks, on the circular path that leads back to the bridge, though they come into view, once their small heads have reared above the long grass, almost as soon as you cross the bridge and turn left. Continue on the main path, ignoring the bridges to the left, closed to the public. After the path curves to the right, it runs straight, with St Catherine's to the left, and eventually passes, on the right, what was once a pond for ornamental and other ducks, with iron gates facing the water-meadow, and a range of golden yews. Years ago this was a luxuriously equipped garden in the otherwise natural scene, and may yet be revived. Carrying straight on over the bridge, however, and ignoring the path past the golden yews to your right, you enter the Fellows' Garden through what will soon again be a grand avenue of Norway maples. Several large stumps of earlier specimens remain, and new ones have recently been planted to match the survivors; there is also a large *Acer cappadocicum* on the right. Further to the right is a glimpse of a meadow with a

18 *Joseph Addison, a Fellow of Magdalen and co-editor of the* Spectator, *inspired the creation of the 'natural' walk alongside the Cherwell, named after him.*

plantation of cricket-bat willows (the blueish *Salix* 'Caerulea'), some of which produced wood for cricket bats, though many have been vandalised.

Now comes a second bridge to be crossed, and a complete change of character. The Fellows' Garden lies ahead, with what amounts to an arboretum including a dawn redwood, two wellingtonias, a lofty ginkgo, firs, pines, cedars, holly, *Cercidiphyllum japonicum* and much more besides. The very large plane that you see from the bridge, by the waterside, may well be the one Oscar Wilde speaks of in his poem 'Magdalen Walks'. (John Heath-Stubbs has a poem, 'Addison's Walk', in *The Heart's Forest*.) In spring the rising and undulating garden is thickly covered with daffodils and anemones. In summer, you can sit by the lily pool at the far end, flanked by lilacs, a weeping pear, roses and a tall cherry, and look down the vista of trees towards the bridge. It is no longer possible to leave here, at the King's Mill, by the door leading towards University Parks, and the only option, pleasant enough, is to stroll back again, preferably by the lower path along the riverside, looking up into the foliage first of the silver lime, then of the copper beech, with the scent of huge philadelphuses wafting along. At the second bridge are two equally agreeable alternatives. Go left past the golden yews where, in winter, you may see redshanks resting. The path will take you almost to Magdalen Bridge before returning you to the main grounds. Or go slightly right, retracing your steps, and there may be a heron, a goldcrest, possibly a kingfisher. This way back is slightly shorter, however, and you may regret that.

19 *Snake's-head fritillaries in Magdalen Meadow, carefully protected for survival.*

Merton College

The Fellows' and Warden's Gardens have been famous for centuries. To reach them, cross aslant Front Quad with its magnolias and enter Fellows' Quad by the arch on the left; here there is another magnolia, a fine *grandiflora*. Emerging on the far side you have in front of you, through the 'water-gate', once needed when floods were frequent, a breathtaking view of Christ Church Meadow. On your left is a gate marked 'Private'; the garden at the end of a short walk is rarely open to the public. If it is not open, there are other gardens which we will visit, but if it is, a few steps will bring us to what was once the Warden's Garden, and is still so called. The wife of a 17th-century Warden, Lady Clayton, had a summer-house here, from which she could overhear the conversation of Fellows as they passed below. Today that has disappeared, but the ancient mulberry (20) at one corner of the lawn was almost certainly planted before her time, in or after 1608, by Warden Sir Henry Savile in response to James I's demand for plantings to create a silk industry. (It is a 'black' mulberry, like all those the King's agent recommended, and would not have produced fine enough silk: only white-fruited ones will do.) The gilt globular sundial was given in 1830.

From the sundial, with your back to the city wall, the view of Champneys' replacement (1904–10) of the medieval St Alban Hall is enhanced by the yellow and red roses and the new mulberry planted along the railing, which you will be looking through from the other side if you come on a non-public day – St Alban's Quad is reached by turning sharp left at the Porters' Lodge. From either angle you will see the rockery, begun in the late 1960s – an innovation needing continual

20 *An ancient 'black' mulberry stands behind the sundial in what was formerly the Warden's Garden of Merton. The steps on the right lead to a walk along the city wall, flanking the college grounds.*

attention from a devoted rock-gardener, and treasured as the gift of Carapiet Balthazar. Full of colour in spring, it has anemones, scillas, aubretia, heathers and both white and purple Pasque flowers. Here the greatest pleasures of the gardens begin: the Fellows' and former Warden's Gardens joined in one, with a low wall that separated them still surviving. Still close to the city wall, steps mount to the terrace (**22**), with a half-round bastion where a culverin was placed in the Civil War. On the garden side of the walk is a *Prunus serrula* 'tibetica' with bark gleaming like burnished copper, and behind the purple lavender a rare *Sorbus aucuparia*, var. 'Xanthocarpa'; a range of maples includes *Acer davidii*, *A. pennsylvanicum*, *A. griseum* and *A. hersii*, planted in 1959, with the silver-grey of *Pyrus salicifolia* ending the vista. Beyond these trees, which will remain low enough as they mature not to obstruct the view, is the famous Lime Walk, a double row of fifteen trees that gives its special character to the Fellows' Garden. There may once have been a bowling alley here. But to see the limes in all their beauty, walk on to the corner and take a few steps along the eastern terrace (shown in Loggan's print of 1675). Looking back down between the limes, planted perhaps about 1740, in succession to an older avenue, you are looking down a slope where until between 1850 and 1875 steps led into the Walk, and in summer nothing could be more invitingly leafy, while in spring the light is yellow with daffodils. A herm given in 1965 suitably terminates the double

21 *The autumn colour of Japanese maples brightens Merton Grove, once a popular meeting-place for town and gown.*

row of gnarled trunks: a 19th-century copy of a sculpture with a Janus-head of Epicurus and his associate Metrodorus, it is a well-placed reminder of the philosophy that pleasure is the chief good.

Ahead is a chaste summer-house of 1706–7, renovated in 1986, at present used as a music room. The city wall still lies on your right; overhung with aubretia and a bushy, dangling *Cotinus coggygria*, it supports a fruit-bearing fig and a *Cytisus battandieri*. Beyond lies the garden of the Rose Lane buildings, where a 'Lady Hillingdon' rose grows against the wall of the garden of the Warden's modern lodgings, and the nursery. Turn left down into the main garden again, where a fine herbaceous border mixed with shrubs, one of the best in Oxford, stretches the whole length of the outer wall on the north side. Of the many plants beyond the path running behind it, *Fritillaria persica* 'Adiyaman' is seldom seen elsewhere.

The old profusion of trees has gone. Williams's print of 1733 indicates almost a forest here, and so lends weight to the poem of 1717 which maintains Merton Walks were thronged with young women in search of a likely husband, though by 1723 they had, it seems, moved to Magdalen. The yew surrounded by a circle of paving was planted as recently as 1932, but the group of three sycamores may be approaching their third centenary. The sycamore standing alone was planted in 1705, and had in 1985 a girth of 11 feet 2 inches (340cm). It was a favourite of the novelist J.R.R. Tolkien. Near to it is a little *Cornus mas* that is a delight as early as February.

Before you return to the 'water-gate', look back and take in the vista now opened up of Magdalen Tower, that constant eye-catcher in all this part of Oxford. William Harvey, the discoverer of the circulation of the blood, must have seen it like this during his brief wardenship of Merton, as must T.S. Eliot, a student here. Today, for those who have the great pleasure and privilege of seeing it, it is a place in which to think approvingly of Epicurus.

If, however, you are not able to visit the private garden, you will have come no further than the 'water-gate', from which you can turn right past the clematis, leaving the Meadow on your left. Within a few yards you enter a garden that has been in existence since about 1320, and was still known in 1701 as the Kitchen Garden, though it no longer grows vegetables. In 1318 Edward II gave the college a strip of land inside the city wall on condition it was never built upon or the city's defences weakened. It is now a pleasant lawn with a dawn redwood planted in 1963 and a giant chestnut which a boring has shown to be two hundred years old. The first of the railings topped with metal pine-cones was erected in 1817.

Further westward lies Butterfield's mid-Victorian addition to the buildings, occupying a part of the ancient Merton Grove, once the site of Goter Hall and now lying obscured. The Grove has been open to the public since 1727; for many years it was a favourite public promenade, broad and spacious, with a 'handsome Gravel-Walk and good flourishing Elms'. The once huge elms died before the elm disease of the 1970s, and the public can now only pass between narrow railings. However, despite the intrusion by Butterfield a great deal is being done to make the walk a pleasant one. In spring the Grove is filled with daffodils, bluebells, and the blossoms of many cherries planted between 1950 and 1966; autumn colour should soon be increased by new plantings of Japanese maples (**21**) including the very rare *Acer triflorum* and the brilliant *A. palmatum* 'Heptalobum Osakazuki'. Beside the Grove is a simple, moving monument to Andrew Irvine, who perished near the summit of Everest in 1924. It has noble lettering by Eric Gill.

From here a turn to the right takes you past the chapel, begun just before 1290, and the library, the oldest part of which dates from 1371-9, through Mob Quad, the oldest in Oxford, to the Porters' Lodge.

New College

There is almost a history of English gardening to be gleaned here. (A pamphlet is obtainable at the Porters' Lodge near Holywell Street.) Coming in from New College Lane you enter Founder's Quad (the oval lawn introduced here in 1789, the camellia and *Magnolia* x *soulangiana* planted after 1920), and turning left enter the peace of William of Wykeham's cloister (**24**), a sheltered walk originally meant for processions and exercise. Most notable around the lawn of this one-time burial ground are the huge ilex in one corner, honeysuckles, and a rose from which Florence Nightingale is said to have plucked a spray.

Coming back through the main quad, going eastwards past the chapel and the dining hall, you enter the three-sided Garden Quad, and here the prospect changes dramatically. Until 1711 a high wall with even higher pedimented gate shut off all view of the garden beyond, except for the tops of trees. The college was one place, the garden another. In that year Thomas Robinson installed the wonderful wrought-iron screen, 130 feet long, which stood until the present deceptively good replica was made in 1894. The whole scene lies open as though on a theatre stage, the slim railings giving at once a view and an enticement to move on into the garden.

The effect of a stage set is partly due to the long perspective of the high-battlemented city wall (begun in 1226) running down the left side, partly to the fantastic mound in the middle, and the distant prospect of Magdalen Tower over more battlements to the right. The magnificent mixed border, a hundred yards long, could have no better setting (**23, 25**). But as in all old Oxford gardens,

35

the effect is due more to time and chance than to long-term planning. This section of city wall has been part of the college since its foundation in 1379, and maintained to this day. The Mound, or Mount as it always used to be called, was first referred to in 1594, when it was fashionable to build such ornaments. As Francis Bacon said of his ideal garden, 'I wish also, in the very middle, a fair mount, with three ascents, and alleys, enough for four to walk abreast . . . the whole mount to be thirty foot high' – which is very much what was erected here. Completed in 1649, its summit, referred to in 1710 as 'Parnassus', served as a place from which to survey the fields and hills outside, as a hiding-place for sportsmen with guns, and as a vantage point for looking down on the floral arms of William of Wykeham and of Charles I, as well as the labyrinthine knot and floral clock that once occupied the sunken area between the Mound and the college. In the Civil War it may have been adapted as a gun emplacement. When Celia Fiennes visited it in 1694 it had a summer-house and perhaps a figure of Time as a weathercock; Williams's print of 1732 seems to show its slopes faced with stone. But the 18th century saw a decline. The floral parterre was abandoned at about the time of the French Revolution, and Romantic ideas took over. The ziggurat shape of the old Mound, with its pyramidal trees dotted in straight lines like wooden soldiers, became more rounded; a serpentine walk replaced the earlier cypresses and pleached limes. But even a wilderness needs maintaining, and the Mound gradually fell into a state of collapse. Self-sown sycamores began to take over, and it was not until after 1945 that the job of restoration was begun.

Lord David Cecil's proposal to re-create the 17th-century 'ziggurat' was not adopted, and the Mound (**26**) is still a mound rather than a model castle. Today there are on the lower slopes daffodils, spurges, hosta, mullein, weigela, alchemilla,

23 *Achillea, mullein, sunflowers and acanthus are sheltered by the medieval city wall that extends along the main part of New College Gardens.*

24 *The branches of a holm oak spread across a large part of the garden of the medieval cloister of New College.*

philadelphus, *Cotinus coggygria*, with holly, lilac, laburnum, rosebay willowherb, *Prunus cistena*, sweet chestnut and oak higher up. From below, the ilex planted in the early 19th century is still the most impressive feature.

From the screen, go round the walls (starting on the left) with their achilleas, delphiniums, and a profusion of other flowers, notably the large catmint, *Nepeta* x *faassenii* 'Six Hills Giant'. At the end of the Garden Quad building is a magnificent wisteria planted about 1830, only fourteen years after the first to be introduced to England. Half-way along the north border is a roomy bastion, with a comfortable seat, and another at the far end. Behind the Mound are horse chestnuts, underplanted with winter aconites, grape hyacinths and daffodils. Here you can turn left through a gate in the city wall, to face the staring eye of Barbara Hepworth's sculpture, acquired in 1964. Beyond is the new Sacher Building for graduate students, but this is private. Returning through the gate from the Hepworth sculpture, you re-enter the main garden at one of its most delightful spots. The back of the Mound is close to you, and there is more Romantic charm about the glade, where you may find students rehearsing a play or studying. To the south the large bay added in the 17th century is almost a separate garden, secluded from the dramatic splendour of the rest, where there are a chestnut, and a venerable tulip tree and a riven copper beech (girths 5 feet 6 inches (168cm) and 8 feet 1 inch (246cm) already in 1912). This part, still beneath battlemented walls, was an orchard before the college bought it from Magdalen. In the 17th century it was used for bowls, as Loggan's print of 1675 shows, 'and round it a Close shady walke, walled round and a Cutt hedge to the bowling-green', as Celia Fiennes wrote twenty years later. Here stands perhaps the finest tree in the gardens, a

London plane, descended from the one raised in the Botanic Garden in the 1660s.

There is more to see if you come on one of the rare days when the Warden's Garden is open to the public under the National Gardens Scheme (entrance in New College Lane). Little is Romantic here except the stable door of the Warden's Barn, built in 1402 (horses were originally kept in the area now a garden), and the fact that little has changed since Warden Nicholas (1675–9) erected a high wall all round it. Judging by the *Oxford Almanac* of 1769 it has very much the same appearance today as it had in the 18th century, including the plain but pretty summer-house of about 1720. There are spaliered pears, also apples, medlars and cherries, a herbaceous border, and a very Romantic overgrown stone stair leading to the Warden's bridge over the lane, by which he can regain the main part of the college. A weeping pear answers the summer-house at the other end, and along the whole length All Souls and Hertford look down enviously, having scarcely any garden of their own.

The Queen's College

One could enter and leave the Queen's College without realising that it has gardens, though it has, some exceptionally beautiful. A glimpse of the Provost's Garden is caught as you enter the walled path by the library. It is normally private, open to the public only when the college dramatic society, the Eglesfield Players, is allowed to stage a production in it. To find it, go through Front Quad and bear left. The Nuns' Garden is through the second gate to the left at the end of a long narrow path with grey limestone and ivy-leaved toadflax either side. Although the

25 *Dahlias cluster between Michaelmas daisies and phlox in the superb mixed border beneath the city wall in New College garden.*

Pre-Raphaelite painting *Convent Thoughts* by Charles Allston Collins in the Ashmolean may enter your mind here, there seems never to have been a nunnery in this part of Oxford, and it is not impossible that a Nunn was the owner.

The garden itself is well suited for meditation. A low doorway in the wall gives on to long narrow beds, full of irises, later of roses and begonias, surrounding a sundial; looking back along the length of the wisteria you see the ancient brewhouse roof beyond. Only a few yards separate you from the High, yet noise is shut out, thanks to the house named after William of Drogheda, a 13th-century canon lawyer, author of what has been called 'the most thoroughly and scandalously unethical legal text-book ever written', who lived just about here. Drawda Hall and the peaceful Little Drawda Garden (**28**), opening out from the Nuns' Garden, were acquired by Queen's only in 1908: the garden is now filled with roses, among which the American eagle of the memorial, intended as an allusion to the name of the college founder, Robert de Eglesfield, stands out in bold contrast. In one corner is a broken piece of statuary, once in the pediment of the north range of Front Quad, now under the branches of a great holm oak hanging over from the Fellows' Garden, which dovetails with this one.

The Fellows' Garden, to the east, usually open once a year under the National Gardens Scheme, has a distinctive character. The quarter-circle of perron under the holm oak makes a perfect stage for dramatic performances. In the wall are a sculptured head of Justitia, a pair of scales and a bowl of fruit, preserved when the pediment in Front Quad was repaired. In the corner furthest from the entrance is a medieval carving of a rebus representing the name Robert Langton of Winchester (a wine barrel for Wine-tun-ensis, and similarly for his other names). It is the only piece of stonework surviving from the college's medieval buildings.

28 *Among the roses of Queen's quiet and formal Little Drawda Garden rises an eagle, an allusion to the name of the college's founder, Robert de Eglesfield.*

Opposite is a stone wall, backing on to the path, which until about twenty years ago had a brick lining providing an inner space along its whole length, which could be heated by a furnace at one end, providing warmth for fruit trees that stood in front. Unfortunately the lining fell in both before and after expensive repairs, and no trace of it now exists.

St Catherine's College

The gardens are unique in Oxford, having been designed by the architect, Professor Arne Jacobsen, down to individual trees and shrubs. (An excellent guide is obtainable at the Porters' Lodge.) Only the basic skeleton of the design exists today, most of the original trees and shrubs having been replaced owing to problems of drainage, top soil and settlement, but the physical linking of the buildings and gardens remains, and the contrast with all other college gardens is striking. Despite the modernity of the buildings, the layout has an unforced symmetry of a classical character, unlike the traditional Oxbridge pattern of quadrangles leading from one to another. The means by which the gardens and landscaping establish links not only between the buildings but also with the past are ingenious.

27 *The brilliant red of geraniums stands out boldly against the 18th-century buildings of Queen's Second Quad.*

The approach is slightly awkward: the road from Nappers Bridge beside the Cherwell runs past the circular bicycle park (clad in firethorn) and the back wall of the Master's Lodgings (with well-labelled climbing roses). A turn to the left brings the four-hundred-foot frontage of the main building suddenly into view, with a

41

path leading across an extremely long lawn parallel to the building and a bridge over the parallel moat (**33**) beyond. There is an austere grandeur about this, and the classical note is accented by Barbara Hepworth's sculpture, *Achaean* (**29**). The terrace on which you now stand has a wall to the right suggesting battlements and a semicircular bastion, rather like those of the city walls, extending to the distant tower of the Music House. Also to the right is a group of three Dawyck beeches that promise in time to provide a strong vertical to answer what is at present the single accent of the belfry tower. Ornamental grasses flank either side of the bridge, another firethorn climbs the walls, and water-lilies (**31**) give shade to shoals of golden orfe. In this long parade of grass and building, with its hint of fortifications, there is something of the sense of entering a defended place that associates the college with many other college buildings in Oxford.

Through the entrance lies a great disc of grass enclosed by low buildings. It makes the first really Scandinavian note, and the verticality of the two cedars of Lebanon keeping each other company only increases the sense of solitude. Here Oxford quadrangles are far from one's thoughts; it is not a place to linger in. Another turn to the left brings you to one of the devices for humanising the scale: short parallel yew hedges line the wall, allow you to pass between them, or outside them, and at the same time suggest a planted equivalent to the brick-work. Similarly the private area is shut off not by a metal gate but by a waist-high Chinese juniper with a young *Magnolia kobus* beyond it.

Retracing your steps to the central quadrangle, and turning left, you meet in autumn a warmth of colour from the Virginia creeper on the wall of the dining hall. As you turn left again out of the central area, the motif of parallel walls is taken up once more, and now they are devised not only to create small enclosed gardens with

30 *The architect Arne Jacobsen's designs link the gardens of St Catherine's with his buildings. Here the low walls, which provide areas for clematis, span the space between the higher walls of residential quarters.*

29 *Barbara Hepworth's sculpture,* Achaean, *stands near the entrance to St Catherine's College, with the Music House in the distance.*

a mulberry, a *Koelreuteria paniculata* and some maples, but also to provide seats outside the Junior Common Room. JCR and SCR are thus linked in external appearance as they are in fact internally.

31 *Water-lilies in the long moat at St Catherine's.*

To reach a really large garden, go past the central lawn southwards, to where the parallel walls of brick are interleaved with walls of yew, followed a few yards further south by walls of yew only. In this way a transition is made from built walls to living walls, and the excitingly planted squares and rectangles of garden now stretch between the buildings almost to the far end. Careful selection provides early blossom in magnolias and tree peonies, *Eucryphia* x *nymansensis* for August, another *Koelreuteria* that will produce long panicles of yellow fruit in late summer, a medlar and *Ptelea trifoliata* for autumn colour, and autumn berries from barberries and *Euonymus* bushes.

Trees are so plentiful here that the route map in the guide is indispensable. At the far end are other features: a paved area with heathers including the interspersed shrub *Erica arborea*, a terrace, and, just to your right at the end, an amphitheatre of yew hedging (**32**) with a vine on the end wall opposite. Beyond the amphitheatre is an area full of trees and shade, where nature takes over completely. A whitebeam, a Judas Tree, liquidambars, incense cedars, Leyland cypresses and black cottonwoods with their distinctive characters give that extraordinary satisfaction that comes from being alone among trees. There are also two dawn redwoods here that will one day, like the Dawyck beeches outside, answer the vertical emphasis of the belfry tower from a closer position.

Between the tower and the western line of buildings is another delightful maze of shrubs and grass lawns, winter-flowering witch hazel, another magnolia, and an already huge *Hydrangea petiolaris* climbing the wall of the private MCR Garden, mercifully also hiding the blotched metal of the wall-covering. Cutting across the south-west corner is the slope of the 'ravelin' or earthwork thrown up in 1642 to defend the ford at Holywell Mill, downstream on the Cherwell. At the end of this line is an extremely colourful array of rock roses, pinks, saxifrages, ferns, along the path to the polygonal Music House. When lit at night by down-pointing lamps two feet above the ground they have an effect like a box of coloured candies. Along the foot of the Music House run the tangled roots of *Peltaphyllum peltatum*, almost invisible once the large leaves appear.

From here the path along the lower garden leads past a Nootka cypress on the left with its crozier head, past the 'bastion' and willows, weeping or purple-stemmed, back to the starting-point. It is all suddenly rustic: the swans sailing down the Cherwell, chub, roach and perch attracting the early morning heron or kingfisher, swallows in the evening swirling round your feet.

St Hilda's College

As you come through the modest entrance there is scarcely a hint of the riverside gardens that make St Hilda's rival the best in Oxford. Turn right, and a first vista opens: a lawn with two great cedars, the more distant one a particularly noble tree, and by the nearer cedar, not far from the holly, an uncommonly large lilac, thought to have been brought back from Asia Minor in 1786 and by college tradition the oldest of its variety still existing in England. Beyond this the lawn slopes down delightfully to the Cherwell and a herbaceous border, fenced with chestnut paling.

32 *A curve of clipped yew frames St Catherine's garden auditorium.*

In wealthier days a handsome railing ran here – remaining sections still stand for some sixty feet in the far corner and are worth looking for. The oval motif on them exactly repeats the motif on the no less handsome Robert Adam staircase in Cowley House (*c.* 1780), which overlooks the garden here, and is evidently part of a design linking the house and garden. We owe this elegance to Humphrey Sibthorp as we owe the lilac to his son John, who was a great traveller and collector.

We return now to the building opposite the entrance, dividing the gardens in two. To its left is a sloping ramp, a vestige of the ford that was once in use, above which rises the pleasing pillared frontage by Sir Albert Richardson. From here begins a view unmatched anywhere. The Cherwell curves away south to a distant Lombardy poplar. Sloping up from the bank is a terraced garden with a path running between daffodils, white, yellow and red broom, saxifrages, primulas, peonies, tulips and quince, a well-maintained rock-garden with violas, thrift, aubretia and rock roses. From a convenient semicircular seat you can watch boys playing cricket across the river, or contemplate in winter the array of colleges from Christ Church to Magdalen, not visible once the leaves appear. The seat is overshadowed by a crab given in honour of Rosalyn Tureck, the distinguished musician and an Honorary Fellow. Nowhere in Oxford is the riverside gardened to such effect; the scene has not changed much since 1932 when Eleanour Sinclair Rohde, a former tutor, described it in her book *Oxford's College Gardens.*

Beyond the next cedar – there are six in the grounds – lies a garden not now at its best, a circle of wallflowers (later phlox) and benches surrounding a bird-bath. This is an invitingly secluded spot, potentially quite glorious in its ring of colour.

Still further along the river lies a water-meadow that claims to rival Magdalen's

33 *The stark geometry of the architecture of St Catherine's is softened by overhanging* Tamarix pentandra *and* Cotinus coggygria.

34 *Roses in St Hilda's. Across the Cherwell is Magdalen College School cricket ground.*

OVERLEAF
35 *A view of the Cherwell where it flows past St Hilda's, with the Milham Ford Building in the background. One of the fords from which Oxford derives its name crossed the river here.*

for fritillaries in May. Used for staging plays in summer, it floods in winter, though the college grounds rise too high to be affected. It could make a pleasant conclusion to walk on from here to the Christ Church ferry leading to Christ Church Meadow, but the peppercorn rent for the St Hilda's meadow does not include this privilege. Return then, taking in the Scots pines and cedars outside the Principal's Lodgings, the great copper beech outside Garden Buildings across the wide lawn, and the prospect of white-pillared Milham Ford Building rising out of the river at the far end of the terrace (**35**). Few colleges have made so much out of so little space.

St Hugh's College

There is not one garden here, but at least nine, and to appreciate their layout some history helps. If you come in by the Porters' Lodge, passing straight through the main building you emerge on a broad, wide terrace full of candytuft, pinks, lamb's ears, *Santolina chamaecyparissus*, alchemilla and, for vertical emphasis, *Sisyrinchium*. In the centre stands a sundial in memory of a great fighter for women's rights, Annie Rogers, also known as Oxford's Gertrude Jekyll. St Hugh's originally admitted only women, and in 1916, when the first St Hugh's building was begun, women were still struggling for 'degrees by degrees', to quote the title of Miss Rogers's autobiography, and as for gardens, there was little money available for them. Her remedy was to raid the men's colleges armed with an umbrella into which she popped cuttings of the plants she most fancied. In the 1930s, her rock-garden had nearly forty varieties of rock roses, largely from St John's, displaying a jewelled variety that would have delighted the Pre-Raphaelites, of

whom she was a great admirer. Like some other Oxford rock-gardens, this one has had to yield to other interests, and the efforts of the present head gardener, John Brooke, successor to George Harris, who served for some sixty years, are bent towards all-the-year-round colour.

Standing by the sundial and looking out over the great lawn, bounded by the small wood on the south side (much as Gertrude Jekyll would have liked), there is still more abundance. Over to the left is a *Magnolia x soulangiana* (**36**), presented by undergraduates in memory of the Armistice of 1918. Near it is a Judas Tree, answering the magnolia's pink-white blossoms with its own profusion of mauve-purple. A rarity nearby is a Judas Tree with white blossoms, still quite young. Also worth seeing slightly later in the year is the *Aesculus parviflora*, a large shrub covered with large chestnut candles, despite the belittling name. Still further over to the left is an 'ordinary' but very big chestnut, whose three trunks appear to divide at ground level – according to one old gardener we do not see the half of this part, since the tree was planted in a small hollow, later filled in.

From the chestnut, which stands between the path and Banbury Road, continue along the 'nut-walk' through the wood, underplanted with spring flowers again in the Jekyll manner. Or, if you keep to the north side of the wood, nearer the main building, you will come across an interesting hybrid, *Crataegomespilus*, a cross between a hawthorn and a medlar, with small medlar-like fruits. Next to this is a crab, *Malus* 'John Downie', one of the best for fruiting. And for comparison a 'common or garden' variety of medlar stands where the path through the nut-walk emerges, at the western end, next to a *Parrotia persica*.

Go back along the south side of the small wood to 'The Lawn', whose front garden contains a snowy mespilus that for some people really makes a spring, and a tall maple, *Acer dasycarpum* (or *saccharinum*), one of America's finest autumn-colouring trees. Then retrace your steps to the wide lawn, once the back garden of the house, with the brick stable now used by the gardeners. From here you look into the back gardens of houses along Canterbury Road that have gradually been assimilated into the college.

From the medlar and parrotia a path leads alongside a row of beeches, dating from 1800, and continues towards the library and the 'Hollow' or Dell, one of the most beautiful parts of the whole garden. Once part of the garden of a house called 'The Mount', earlier a gravel pit, this has a rose pergola, a small pool fed by running water and overhung with ferns, and a winding path that makes it all feel very Victorian. There is also an unusual maple, *Acer spicatum*, with rather small delicately pointed leaves, also providing rich autumn colours. At the entrance to the Dell is a strange waisted stone, apparently placed by a private owner in the last century: sarsen stone? mother goddess? a rejected embryo meant for the Sheldonian's collection of gigantic heads?

From here it is possible to take in some of the wealth of climbing plants and shrubs stretching all along the face of the older buildings, notably the *Magnolia grandiflora* in the north-east corner of the terrace garden, which has reached the roof and produces its great white blooms in profusion. Along or on the walls are *Itea ilicifolia*, with long green-white racemes like catkins, the 'Chinese gooseberry' (*Actinidia chinensis*) and the beautiful *Parthenocissus henryana* on the Wolfson Building, at the western end of the college.

From the Dell you can also see the herbaceous border set with half-standard apple trees between the main building and the projecting library, as well as the open space to the west, with another magnolia, a wild and a bird cherry together with a Japanese one, *Prunus* 'Ichiyo' (*serrulata unifolia*). Beyond these to the south are the Fellows' Garden and Principal's Garden, open on specified days under the

36 *A* Magnolia x soulangiana *blooms in St Hugh's Garden, commemorating the Armistice of 1918.*

National Gardens Scheme. Also inherited from earlier owners, the Fellows' Garden is still being improved, and the terrace garden, old orchid greenhouses, and string of deep pools for irises are gradually being revived after the final disappearance of wartime hospital wards from this area.

Striking north again and passing through the nursery beds and narrow avenue of apples, behind the balconied Kenyon Building, you reach 'K.K. Leung House' (1883) on the corner of St Margaret's Road, once owned by Gilbert Murray, with its sunken sloping garden. From here, there is an interesting walk eastwards between the road and the Wolfson Building. The boomerang-shaped pool was recently planted with water-lilies and other aquatic plants. Immediately facing it is an unusual feature, a paved area suggesting quincunxes, or five-of-diamond crosses, planted with cockspur thorns – this would have delighted Sir Thomas Browne, who in *The Garden of Cyrus* advocated the quincunx as not only the most rational of layouts but also, being cross-like, the most satisfying symbolically.

The narrow path between the walls and the thick shrubbery is brightened by a *Prunus* 'Kanzan', and a 'Ghost' or 'Handkerchief Tree', *Davidia vilmoriniana*, half-way along, with a profusion of white blossoms in spring. Near the end of the path, close to the Porters' Lodge, is a fine silver birch.

St John's College

These are by repute among the best gardens in the university, and although in the last few decades there have been some changes, not least the removal of a great many elms, this has had less effect than might be expected. After recent plantings, they are the richest in colour of any in Oxford.

The garden was designed by neither 'Capability' Brown nor Humphrey Repton, something of a distinction in itself. The peaceable great lawn with symmetrically placed copper beeches narrowing the vista in the distance was once the formally laid-out Master's Garden, while the wooded area to the left was the equally formal Fellows' Garden, separated by a wall until 1777. A move along the path to the left allows a sideways look back at the beautiful garden front of the library (**40**), with shrubs either side of the entrance answering the symmetry of the copper beeches in the far distance and of the front itself. To the right is a promising young *Cornus controversa* 'variegata', with light green foliage on horizontal branches.

Further to the left is the celebrated rock-garden, where there is a tablet to the Bursar, H.J.Bidder, who in 1913 published a printed list of nearly seven hundred mainly Alpine plants then growing here. Every variety of Alpine pink was to be found, nearly every variety of *erodium*, with Himalayan poppies, brooms from Dalmatia and the Shipka Pass, the mauve *Raymonda pyrenaica*, and a *Saxifrage cotyledon (Norvegica)* brought back by one of the Fellows from Iceland. Eighty-eight saxifrages alone are listed. Sadly, like all rock-gardens, this needed unremitting attention from an enthusiast, and for a while it did not prosper. In 1986, however, it was reconstructed on an impressive scale and largely replanted by R. Whitelegg.

Recently most work has gone into clearing away from the west end of the former Fellows' Garden the dense shrubbery of twelve-foot high privet and other rampant growths. The big weeping beech facing the rock-garden has been provided with an embracing semicircle of yew and golden yew hedge and a collection of roses. A newly planted cut-leaved beech and other new trees near the path should not obtrude on this welcome.

37 *The jagged leaves of the poisonous giant hogweed spread near the centre of St John's Fellows' Garden.*

Yet most of the garden on this side is still hidden, to be reached by following the path as it curves to the right. Only gradually does the full impression reveal itself: at first, past the north end of the yew hedge, a pair of old yews screen the view, though a glimpse is had of the weeping beech and cut-leaved beech (**39**) – perhaps the finest tree in the garden – on the further side. As you leave the path at the holm oak, the plan becomes clearer. There is a large open glade, as there has been for at least fifty, perhaps four hundred years, and a great variety of young trees overlooked by a fine old *Pinus wallichiana*, or Bhutan pine. These, with the bluebells now being naturalised, are part of a plan to create an effect of woodland. A humbler plant is the elder, a great attraction to bluetits and tomtits and a reminder that the garden has some claim to being a bird sanctuary for blackcaps, nuthatches, chaffinches, wrens, coal-tits and the four robins who divide the five acres of the whole between them. Also humble in a way is the clump of giant hogweed (**37**), carrying its superb broad umbels eight feet above the ground, but seasonally roped off, with a large notice warning visitors against irritation caused by touching the plants.

At this point seats along the path afford views between the fastigiate Arizona cypresses and fastigiate beeches of the central lawn, covered in early spring with crocuses. The winding path to the terrace behind the seats, an area formerly grassed over, is gradually taking on a pleasant woodland character. At the north

This cut-leaved beech is perhaps the finest tree in St John's.

end is a seat, from which you can look down an avenue crammed with brilliant yellow daffodils, cowslips and primroses in spring, peonies, marigolds, yellow and orange Welsh poppies, orange day-lilies in summer. The colours here are luxurious, intense, including the red of camellias, yellow and red crown imperials, gorse, purple heather, white hyacinths, forsythias, reminiscent on some days of Monet's paintings of his garden at Givency. Of the trees here a sea buckthorn (*Hippophaë rhamnoides*) near the southern end is worth looking for, with silver-grey leaves and long thorns.

At the end of the woodland walk you can go back up the northern side of the great lawn, or carry on to the walk along the wall adjoining Trinity's garden. The former will take you to a sight unusual in Oxford, rhododendrons (**38**), including *R. ciliatum*, rather small, blossoming in March and April, and the superb *R. loderi* 'King George', blossoming later. These are made possible by deep pits of peat dug at intervals since the 1930s. Similar pits have been dug more recently for lilies and camellias. *Styrax japonica* here, known to Americans as 'snowbells', is uncommonly beautiful in flower.

38 *St John's magnificent rhododendrons thrive in deep pits of peat, providing Oxford with flowers seldom seen elsewhere in the city, because the local soil has too much free lime.*

Alternatively, go on to the south-east corner, where there are more new conifers, pausing on the way to take in the great sea of lawn with the low library building beyond. On the return path is a fairly rare Indian chestnut, badly damaged by the frosts of 1981, though a replacement is already growing further along. On the wall side are two ancient holm oaks that were almost lost after the same frosts, but made a marvellous recovery. As insurance against a relapse, two hawthorns, a holly and a cedar of Lebanon have recently been planted.

The path leads back to the gate into Canterbury Quad, after which a turn to the left from Front Quad brings you eventually to Dolphin Quad, unremarkable except for two mulberries, one of them quite old, while a turn to the right from Front Quad brings you past the celebrated 'Beehive' buildings with their chestnut, to the Sir Thomas White Building, where all the planting (except for the mulberry) has been done in the last ten years. A half-circle of columnar trees forms a group looking at Arup Associates' buildings, and a *Fraxinus oxycarpa* 'Raywood' is worth seeing in autumn for its plum-purple foliage. The cedar of Lebanon near the end of the path leading into the building has the added interest that it was bought from the garden of Agatha Christie in Devonshire. As you leave the college at this end, the very old horse chestnut on the way to the Lamb and Flag is bound to catch the eye. Small leaves sprout from all over the bole, while the crown is still massive and healthy.

Somerville College

The dainty Darbishire Quad, at the Woodstock Road entrance, is in a 'Cotswold' style of 1690, though built in 1933, with a low terrace, its grey walls enlivened with wisterias, *Hydrangea petiolaris*, *Pyrus salicifolia*, three fastigiate cherries, tulips, geraniums and roses. Its small size and low archway, leading through a wasteland of parked cars to a second arch, makes Garden Quad beyond seem all the more expansive. In April massed daffodils under the lime surround a sculpture (*Elipsodrome*, 1963, by Werthman), followed in May by flowering cherries veiling in white a zig-zag of near-triangles (*Triad*, by Wendy Taylor), later still by several wisterias and two *Magnolia grandiflora* gracing the entrance to the red-brick 'Queen Anne' library. In front of this stands an Atlantic cedar planted in 1976 by the Visitor of the college, Harold Macmillan. Other trees include a young mulberry, a tulip tree and a cherry whose globular form would have pleased Samuel Palmer. Near this, on the opposite side of the quad from the library, a row of Lombardy poplars and a beech hedge screen off the private Fellows' Garden, facing which is an unusual feature, a garden with a catalpa, reserved for graduate students.

Trinity College

The first impression from Broad Street is mixed. Two tall silver birches that would grace any heathland stand next to two noble pillared columns with urns, while alongside stand the humble, carefully preserved cottages housing the Porters' Lodge, too lowly in their own beauty to look quite right next to the palatial gateway. The path leading through Front Quad (**41**) has a similarly mixed character: ahead lies the stately chapel, once attributed not unworthily to Wren, but there is no avenue, even though this path once ran between two close-set walls. Beyond the walls to the east there was an orchard, and a gnarled apple tree is still tucked away in the broad expanse. But the whole lawn is a scatter of great trees, no longer forming three sides of a square (as in New's engraving of 1933), more like an unusually varied wood than a planned accompaniment to the buildings. Two youngish cedars do line the path, and there is plenty of shade from the plane, the silver birch, the oak and the laburnum. These hide from the passer-by some superb hydrangeas on the building beyond. The venerable forked catalpa in the middle is thought to be one of the first planted in England (introduced 1726), although the date may be 1803 rather than 1737.

40 *The 16th-century library front of St John's overlooks the brilliant senecio of the Fellow's Garden.*

Walk on past the *Malus hupehensis*, all alone on the left of the path, through the gate tower next to the chapel, and you enter Durham Quad, named after the earlier Durham College. About 1980 the gravel covering here was replaced by the fine rippled paving stones, deep red after rain, bought from the city of Bradford, and the octagonal raised lawn. Next comes the handsome Garden Quad, surrounded on three sides by a building originally Wren's; the four elegant 18th-century lead urns form part of a recent gift. The wrought-iron gateway by Seymour Lindsay is a memorial to Trinity men who died in the Second World War, and the red roses beyond, a species named after the popular wartime song *Lili Marlene*, evoke something of the spirit of those days. The quinces spreading along the railings contribute a brighter red in spring.

The view through the railings recalls the one from Garden Quad at New College, but there is no mound or city wall, rather a broad expanse of lawn with a fine, long herbaceous border on one side and the remnants of a yew wall and a famous Lime Walk on the other. It is in some ways like the lawn in the southern half of St John's garden beyond the wall; the whole of both gardens once belonged to the Benedictine monks of Durham College, and there is something of a wide seascape about this lawn too. But time has brought changes. The yews on your right at the end are all that is left of a planting that once enclosed the garden on three sides, 'cut into regular pilasters and compartments' and surprisingly beautiful, as Robert Southey wrote. Efforts are being made to fill the gaps, though not to restore that 19th-century look. Today Cardinal Newman's bust looks down a long vista leading to the splendid gatepiers on Parks Road, dating from 1713.

Enter the garden and turn right to pass the high wall of the President's Garden, possibly built by the Benedictines. Then come the yews, and the Lime Walk, dating from 1713 and possibly suggested by John Evelyn, though the pollarded limes that used to arch together overhead, each one surrounded by a ring of daffodils, are all gone, and the new ones, *Tilia europa*, *T. platyphyllos*, *T. petiolaris* and, most recently, the smaller *T. mongolica*, have yet to reach maturity. (In the nearby glade, however, there are still both overarching boughs and daffodil rings, and many other spring flowers well worth a visit.) One plan for the Walk is to set the bust of Newman as a terminus facing some other sculpture at the opposite end, since the path here also leads nowhere.

In the pleasant shady area between the Lime Walk and the buildings there was once a maze. There was also in the area between the classical library and the back of Sir Thomas Jackson's Tudor Revival buildings a beautiful rose garden, designed by President Weaver. That has gone now, to make room for a paved area with a design covering the new basement of Blackwell's bookshop, a sad loss for the college.

The garden has changed a good deal since the Civil War when it was 'the Daphne [laurel grove] for the Ladies and their Gallants to walke in', and when 'my lady Isabella Thynne (who lay at Balliol College [next door]) would make her entry with a Theorbo or Lute played before her'. Renewals are under way.

Wadham College

The history of these famous gardens is of one long taking down of walls and of providing more and more access, over a period of nearly four hundred years. The two grass plots by the entrance were enclosed by high walls till 1805, and even the railings along Parks Road went in the early years of this century. Front Quad has never had much to show by way of a garden – till 1809 it was all gravel, as some

41 *A handsome cherry in Trinity's tree-filled Front Quad, seen through the wrought-iron gates at the north-east corner.*

Front Quads still are. But go in and turn left for an unforgettable view of what is still called the Fellows' Garden, though used now by all members of the college. It is open to the public in the afternoons.

The most striking feature is the old copper beech (**43**) in the far corner, planted in 1795 – rather a Polyphemus now that one huge branch has gone, leaving a black eye staring out of bare branches that have as yet no foliage on the open side. To your left as you enter is a great conical golden yew almost as tall as the buildings, and a famous cedar shown in the *Oxford Almanack* of 1819, though this too may be in its final years. On the rectangular lawn is a curiosity, *Magnolia acuminata*, the Cucumber Tree (girth in 1985: 6 feet 10 inches (208cm)), with fruits like cucumbers up to 3 inches (8cm) in height. Could this have been brought back from some voyage by Admiral Wills for his brother Warden Wills, late in the 18th century?

At the beginning of Warden Wills's time this garden was still predominantly 17th century in character. There had been a mound like the one at New College, topped by an Atlas carrying a golden globe who must have been visible from far afield until he was blown down in the 1750s. Warden Wilkins, a friend of Sir Christopher Wren and John Evelyn, had also a 'talking statue' (operated by a man speaking down a long, concealed tube), a beehive arranged like a castle, and the

42 *Trinity's Cumberbatch Quad, whose buildings are a mixture of neo-Tudor and 20th century, overlooks the garden near what was once the college's ancient and famous Lime Walk.*

then fashionable topiary and straight lines of pleached trees enclosing summer-houses. The formal garden disappeared when Mr Shipley, gardener at Blenheim, took over in 1795 at Warden Wills's request. How much landscaping Shipley carried out is uncertain. The terrace on the east side of the Fellows' Private Garden and further south may have been built up after 1806 under Warden Tournay; originally it was part of the defences erected by Charles I during the siege of 1642.

Moving clockwise from the golden yew you see first a *Staphylea colchica* or bladdernut, with bladdery fruits, then a dittany plant *(Dictamnus fraxinella)* or 'burning bush', well known for the inflammable vapour it gives off, with startling night-time effects. (Easily recognised: 'out of the middle cometh a tassel of long haires like a beard turning up at the bottom', says an old herbal.) Further round is an *Acer griseum*, with grisly ragged bark which has a fine flaming appearance when seen against the sun. In the far corner is an intriguing looped path with two fine magnolias and an Etna broom – another inflammatory association, since it grows on the slopes of the volcano (which is also the original home of Oxford ragwort). In the next corner the ancient copper beech takes almost all the space; daffodils thrive beneath it. On the lawn stands another cedar, and following the path back towards the college you find another of the rarities, *Phillyrea latifolia*. Close to it a ginkgo rises spindly and extremely tall, as does a Lombardy poplar. A *Cercidiphyllum japonicum* (possibly 'Magnificum', since its branches are not bunched at the base), rather like a Judas Tree but with opposite instead of alternate leaves, shelters the somewhat concealed and controversial statue of Maurice Bowra (Warden 1936–70). The space behind the chapel and the dining hall, the college burial ground until 1777, is now the 'Cloister Garden', the grove beyond which is partly planted as a bluebell wood.

If this is one of the rare days when both the Fellows' Private Garden and the Warden's Garden are open to the public, turn back, past the aged copper beech, and enter the Private Garden, crossing the boundary-line of the medieval Augustinian priory: all beyond was bought in 1795. Below to your right is the dark, confined, aptly named 'Love Lane'. Across the grass are a copper beech, a ginkgo, a *Paulownia*, a mulberry, a medlar and a *Parrotia persica*. To the right, further along below the terrace, are a beautifully formed apple tree, the well-disguised gardener's hut, known as the 'Cow-shed', a quince and a very young copper beech. Somewhere near the north-east corner you may find a roving tortoise, with the college telephone number on his shell. Or he may be in the long memorial border created in 1985 along the north wall, including *Hibiscus syriacus* 'Blue Bird', some fuchsias, many viburnums, and a great many different geraniums, together with three cypresses. A Lucombe oak on the lawn was removed in 1985, having achieved a girth of 10 feet 1 inch (309cm). But the tulip tree planted by Warden Bowra flourishes, as does the Tree of Heaven and the great yew in the south-west corner by the Gothic arch, where pokeweed, looking in autumn like a purple corn-on-the-cob, has managed to find a place.

Another wall has come down here. From this end of the Fellows' Private Garden, as you look straight down to the Warden's Lodgings, note the four-stemmed holm oak (14 feet 3 inches (429cm) round three of the stems in 1985) and the biggest tulip tree in Oxford, three-pronged, with the typical swollen bole or 'elephant's foot' at the bottom, and a waist in 1985 of 13 feet 5 inches (411cm) at 4 feet from the ground. Both these are surely of Warden Wills's planting, and so date from about 1800. At this point you may wish to sit in front of the Lodgings, looking back at the two of them and at the long romantic vista opened up by the 18th-century demolition of part of the priory wall. On the left are the two pretty cottages that face

Parks Road, with rustic roofs just visible. Between the tall planes along the road there is a glimpse of the cross high over Keble library.

On a day when it is not possible to visit these private gardens, go back through Front Quad and out again on the south side to Back Quad. Here there is a Tree of Heaven, and above all a great pendent silver lime of unknown age (11 feet 2½ inches (342cm) girth in 1985), whose scent in summer fills the whole of Parks Road from the Bodleian extension as far as Keble. Bees, finding the same scent fatally irresistible, lie in dozens at its feet.

43 *This great copper beech, nearly two hundred years old, dominates the garden at Wadham still known as the Fellows' Garden.*

Beyond Back Quad lies a charming old yard with a Judas Tree, and the beautiful semicircular apse of Holywell Music Room, with a climbing *Parthenocissus henryana* on the wall, a *Parrotia* that flames red against the white stone in autumn, and a *Euonymus kiautschovicus*. Other rarities planned for these richly endowed grounds include *Eucommia ulmoides* (the 'Gutta Percha' Tree), *Tsuga sinensis* and Jargonelle pears.

Wolfson College

The entrance does not really look like one; it will have more presence when the mature-planted London plane has grown to the height of the already mature chestnut on the opposite side. But the manna ash to the left will help to emphasise the easy-going asymmetry of the whole area, in contrast to the almost palatial front of St Catherine's.

Main Quad still retains the simple formality of a plain and well-kept lawn. But at the far end you emerge into a series of gardens that have developed with extraordinary swiftness. The buildings were formally opened in 1974. What mature trees you see – the Turkey oak to your right, for instance, and the chestnuts towards the left by the bridge – remain from gardens belonging to the Haldane family. But the *Campsis radicans* blowing its own red trumpets on the wall just behind you on your right was planted much less than ten years ago, and so was the golden ivy alongside. The bed at the foot of the wall is full of interesting things: *Photinia fraseri* set with *Dicentra spectabilis* ('Dutchman's breeches') for their contrasting reds, *Poncirus trifoliata*, green and spiny, hybridised to produce the 'citrange' or lemon-orange, *Colquhounia coccinea mollis*, a Himalayan shrub with orange-scarlet flowers, *Clerodendron bungei*, *Daphne pontica* and *Melianthus major*. A *Betula jacquemontii*, with dazzling white stem, stands almost opposite you.

A good deal is being done to hide the car-park. A herbaceous border and shrubbery intervene between it and the croquet lawn to your right, with another border beyond the lawn leading past the garden of the President's house (private, with a tall pear and a tulip tree) towards an area still being developed. A paved pergola has been built at right angles to the path on which you now stand, forming part of the 'Iffley Garden' (behind the greenhouses), where there is to be a sundial with four L-shaped beds. (Iffley College, founded in 1965, became Wolfson College in 1966.) Beyond this is a unique feature – allotments used by Fellows and graduate members for growing vegetables.

Moving eastwards you enter a woodland area with a good deal of interesting underplanting – among others, winter aconite beneath Chinese witch hazel, *Anemone blanda atrocoerulea* beneath the uncommon *Sarcococca ruscifolia* ('Christmas box'), *Incarvillea delavayi* ('Chinese trumpet flower') and *Sycopsis sinensis*. A winding path leads to a view of what will soon be an unusual winter garden.

The gleaming white pinnacle in front of the yew hedge was taken from the top of Merton chapel, Merton College having contributed to the foundation of Wolfson. It is a folly that gives presence to the beds spreading in a curve either side of a large lawn set with hundreds of crocuses, and a *Parrotia* off-centre. In the beds, planted in 1984, are *Cornus alba* 'sibirica' for the bright colours achieved after cutting back, *Rubus cockburnianus*, *Osmanthus yunnanensis*, *Cotoneaster lacteus*, with a profusion of red berries lasting till well after Christmas, many heathers, junipers, skimmias and maples. Still further eastwards it is proposed to leave untouched the lovely natural woodland, where masses of cuckoopint grow under the low-branched chestnuts. After a downward slope, a riverside walk paved with small oblong setts leads to the new 'rainbow' bridge (**44**), like the one in University Parks though less elegant.

A good view of the best part of the buildings can be had from the top of the bridge, but a still better one from within River Quad, preferably from the terrace on the west wall. Thanks to the architects' creation of a 'harbour' closed off from the Cherwell by an island, there is a Mediterranean feeling here on a fine day. The white building curving away on either side, and the places for punts beneath, with a kind of mole running out to the left and a lawn sloping down to it, suggest the South of France. The brilliant white of the snowy mespilus and the narcissi blossoming on the slopes in spring make an all-white response to the white buildings. Beyond, a carefully managed natural scene contrasts with the formality of the lawn. Snake's-head fritillaries have been planted, with three species of alder which will eventually replace some of the less indigenous trees on the island. Water-lilies and reeds are encouraged in the harbour. Volunteers of the college's Linnean Club help to preserve wild flowers, such as the great hairy willowherb, in the meadows beyond. The panorama over the winding river to the distant hills of Beckley completes the scene.

What remains is a slight anticlimax, though a tulip tree and a ginkgo stand in the field to the left of the harbour, which is covered with crocuses and daffodils in spring. Even so, Tree Quad, reached from the field by turning left, is well conceived as a total contrast. The atmosphere of enclosed peacefulness is partly due to the spaced-out mature trees, including a sycamore, a new *Eucalyptus gunnii*, and a most beautiful *Prunus* 'Sargentii'. *Clematis montana* has begun to climb up the pillars to the rather ship-like terrace. The mound leading to this terrace at one end gives the lawn an individual character.

Worcester College

The first view is dramatic: the 18th-century classical buildings on the right of the Quad, raised proudly above a steep lawn, look down on the medieval ones of the former Gloucester Hall, which are mildly unconcerned. Along the wall on the open, western side run a wisteria and a *Campsis radicans*, just allowing a glimpse from the terrace into the Provost's Garden. Above rises a wall of trees answering the buildings with a splendour of its own.

At the far left-hand (south-west) corner is a gate leading to a tunnel beneath the garden of the Vice-Provost (**45**). Traditionally this is the long underground passage leading to 'the loveliest garden you ever saw', along which Alice followed the White Rabbit – there are traces of Alice everywhere in Oxford, and she often fed the ducks on Worcester lake. Follow the tunnel, and you come out into a large arboretum. Look left at the woodwork of the cottage orné, and the huge chimney-breast of the medieval kitchens, with its climbing pink roses.

Some of the trees in the arboretum date back to even earlier than 1827, when the grounds as a whole were laid out. A folder to be had from the Porters' Lodge lists 2 copper beeches and 24 other trees, including a very large catalpa to your left – beans 22 inches (56cm) long – an equally fine tulip tree, and the doyen of them all, a gigantic London plane covering the length of two cricket pitches and dominating the scene. Apparently 12 feet (366cm) in circumference in 1912, it had reached 20 feet 3 inches (617cm) in 1985.

Better known even than the arboretum is the lake (**1**), reclaimed from swamp *c*. 1820, and embodying Alexander Pope's precept for all landscape design, 'the contrasts, the management of surprises, and the concealment of bounds'. It is a kind of Serpentine, and almost as accessible to the public: you will see Oxford city

44 *A 'rainbow' bridge similar to the one in University Parks leads across the Cherwell to Wolfson College.*

45 *This passageway
into Worcester's
quadrangle runs
underneath the garden
of the Vice-Provost.*

anglers here any day, as well as, in the early morning, the odd heron.

On the way to the restored medieval gateway, you pass a plaque in memory of a former head gardner, William George Ward (**46**). Beyond the gateway appear the chestnut and willows, deliberately canted out, looking like bowsprits. Follow the lake round, keeping on your left the Oxford Canal, now lined with long holiday-making barges. For a moment the new Sainsbury Buildings come into view at the far end, as do the water-lilies presented by Lord Nuffield. From here on, careful plantings hide the lake most of the time, allowing only glimpses of it, though the playing fields to the left (trees planted in 1913) are wide open. The gardens of the Sainsbury Buildings have received special attention, each pair of rooms having its own small lawn and Japanese maple or juniper, or balcony box with plants. Heathers have been set between paving stones, and a lower garden at the back is stocked with cherries given by a Japanese student. A low cascade flows between reeds and marsh marigolds, with a curve of brick steps above for seated contemplation, and unusually large circular recesses at the foot of gutters, meant to provide temporary pools in wet weather. With its 'prow' leaning out over the lake, this building is well worth the long walk.

The short-cut back to Front Quad is absolutely private, as is the Provost's formal garden, overlooked by the imposing Palladian front.

46 *William George
Ward retired as head
gardener of Worcester
in 1968. This plaque
gratefully acknowl-
edges his 62 years'
service to the college.*

The Botanic Gardens

A most inviting sight in Oxford on a warm day is the fountain playing in the sun, viewed through the massive stone arch of Nicholas Stone's 17th-century entrance to the main garden. The square of fourteen-foot-high walls over five hundred yards in perimeter was built between 1621 and 1632, enclosing three acres. In winter the parallel rows of systematic beds lend it the aspect of a Roman military camp, to which the entrance, named after the founder, the Earl of Danby, provides a triumphal arch. But the regularity soon gives way to thousands of blooms, and these high walls provide shelter for many non-hardy plants rarely seen outdoors in Britain. The western side, external to the main garden, protects early spring flowers that would suffer damage from early morning sunshine. Some three hundred species and varieties of wall plants grow here, all listed in the official Guide. Not listed, however, are the even more numerous plants in the parallel beds occupying all the central space. There is no better garden in Oxford at any time of the year.

As you enter, more meets the eye than can easily be taken in. Just to the right is a tall feathery swamp cypress, planted in 1840, of which Gunther wrote in 1912, 'the identical tree at Chapultepec under which Montezuma was accustomed to sit previously to the conquest of Mexico is yet living, and known as the Cypress of Montezuma'. It is altogether a better name for this fifty- or sixty-foot royal plume. A few yards east of the central path is a humbler and younger tree, the *Sophora japonica* or Scholar's Tree, the emblem of the academic botanist here and at Cambridge, planted in 1971 by Harold Macmillan, then Chancellor of the University, to commemorate the 350th anniversary of the founding of the garden.

Further down the central path, on the left, is a direct descendant of the Witty (or Whitey) Pear, or True Service Tree *(Sorbus domestica*, f. *pyrifera)* known to Worcestershire men for having once grown in the midst of the Wyre Forest, a sole specimen of unknown origin. Round the fountain (**48**) are four specialities: a well-grown *Koelreuteria paniculata*, a *Fraxinus ornus*, planted about 1790, named the manna ash because of a dried sugary exudation from the stem (not connected with Biblical manna but once used as a children's laxative), the rare *Fraxinus pennsylvanica* or red ash, and the also rare *Sorbus latifolia* or Service Tree of Fontainebleau. The last two were planted in *c*. 1850 and *c*. 1840. The American persimmon nearby *(Diospyros virginiana)* is said to be the largest of its kind in Britain.

There are nearly a hundred and fifty notable trees in the Garden, and the dates of their planting are all given in the official Guide. A few more need special mention, particularly the yew at the far end of the central path (**50**), sole survivor of an avenue of male and female trees facing each other planted *c*. 1650 by the earliest keeper of the Garden, a German ex-soldier and publican called Jacob Bobart. The

47 Lilium tigrinum *(tiger-lily) in one of the Botanic Garden greenhouses.*

last female was blown down in a gale in 1976. The Austrian pine to the left (or south-east) beyond the ancient white mulberry, as well as the *Ginkgo biloba* to the right, near the west wall, are both giant specimens. Smaller but no less interesting is the Glastonbury Thorn (1966) (*Crataegus monogyna* 'Biflora' ('Praecox')), about 30 paces from the Austrian pine on the path parallel to the central path. Traditionally believed to have grown from a flowering walking-stick brought by Joseph of Arimathea from the Holy Land, this always blossomed on Christmas Day, though it delayed till 5 January when the Gregorian calendar was adopted in 1752. A January blossoming can usually be counted on today.

The main object of the Botanic Garden (as distinct from its subsidiary Genetic Garden) is to demonstrate the present end-products of evolution, and this the systematic beds do by their orderly arrangement. Start at the Danby Gate where you came in, and walk to the far left, beyond the sphinx. Omitting the first bed, which has irises, the second is full of the family *Ranunculaceae*, which most people connect with buttercups, one of the most primitive orders of plants. In this and the next beds behind you may find hellebores, columbines, delphiniums, peonies, and lesser celandines, all distinguished by having free petals, i.e. not joined together, and by being dicotyledons, i.e. with twin seed-leaves which fall off early in life.

48 *One of the two splendid ash trees which border the central fountain and pool.*

49 *Autumn colours of a* Parrotia persica, *a native of the region from North Iran to the Caucasus, brighten a corner of the Botanic Garden. It is easily recognised by its long, bare upper branches.*

They are also hermaphrodites, male and female in the same flower.

Southward through the serried ranks new families are named on the metal plaques, expanding and contracting in number through the year as fresh specimens come up or are brought in. Many epimediums illustrate the *Berberidaceae*. *Papaveraceae* include the opium poppy, a reminder of Thomas de Quincey, the 'English Opium Eater', who was for a while at Worcester College, where a bust of him is preserved. The *Cruciferae* follow with such examples as alyssum, and seakale, with its sprays of white blossom six foot high. Carnations figure among the *Caryophyllaceae*, and half a dozen more families follow till the southern boundary is reached after five beds of *Leguminosae*, including lupins and sweetpeas.

Turn right now, and cross the intermediate path to the next legion, starting with *Rosaceae*, and going back towards the Danby Gate to the *Saxifragaceae* and *Cucurbitaceae*, among which are the gourds. These climb poles and dangle heavily in yellow and green lumps, except for the squirting cucumbers, which squirt their offspring (looking rather like Kiwi fruit) several feet the moment they are ripe. Further down are, among others, the *Umbelliferae* – cow-parsnip, sweet Cicely, angelica – easily recognised by their umbrella-like spread.

But come back slantwise to Bobart's ancient yew, by the southern pillar clad in golden ivy, and cross the central path to the *Compositae*, if you want to keep to the Darwinian demonstration. The name of the family indicates that the flowers in it, like the daisy and dandelion, are not solitary, but combined in inflorescences, which represent a higher stage in evolution.

Moving towards the Danby Gate, cross the path near the central fountain, and the plants illustrate evolution into such families as *Primulaceae*, *Gentianaceae* and

Boraginaceae, all with well-known representatives having similar names. Gradually many-parted flowers are succeeded by those with few parts, petalled flowers by flowers having petals united in a tube, or with no petals, and the regular flower by the irregular. Carpels are increasingly fused together, and many-carpelled flowers are followed by those with few carpels, aggregate fruits by single fruits.

So you come to the *Solanaceae*, which include the potato as well as belladonna; the snapdragon family, including foxgloves; and ivy-leaved toadflax as well as antirrhinum; the mint family or *Labiatae*; and finally two beds of variegated plants which have nothing to do with illustrating evolutionary order, being devoted to 'structured patterns' and 'plastid chimaeras', in other words organisms consisting of different tissues, genetically distinct but growing in union side by side, not fused. Turn east past the Danby Gate across the central path and there are more families, mostly *Polygonaceae* and *Euphorbiaceae*. Where the first three 'legions' represented were *Polypetalae*, or many-petalled plants, the second two *Gamopetalae* (united petals), this last one is of *Apetalae*, or flowers with no petals at all, or very inconspicuous ones: docks and sorrels, for instance.

That accounts more or less for all the four sections to the east of the central path, and two of those to the west of it. The two sections further to the west, next to the beds along the wall, contain (after beds showing crosses between genera) first the monocotyledons, then economic and medicinal plants. The monocotyledons, for the most part irises, lilies, garlics or alliums, and grasses, are distinctive – not so much by having one seed-leaf, which you seldom see, as by having leaves with parallel veins (though not in arums) and smooth, not toothed, margins, and by having flowers in which sepals and petals have coalesced. All cereals are

50 *An avenue of yew trees, planted in the late 17th century, once lined the central path of the Botanic Garden. The sole survivor rises beyond a pillar overgrown with golden ivy, as you look back from the New Garden.*

monocotyledons. The economic plants include maize, indigo, mint, sisal; the medicinal include not only herbs – dill, lemon verbena, tarragon, sweet basil, winter savory – but deadly nightshade for belladonna, foxglove for digitalis, *Nicotiana*, and the notorious poison oak that causes a lot more irritation than our native stinging nettles do, as Americans know: a touch is sheer folly. Another bed of euphorbias lies beneath the great ginkgo.

Those are the principal contents between the square walls, apart from the ferns over to the eastern side. But at the southern end of the square the noble pillars mark the entrance to the triangular New Garden. The pond here with water-lilies and goldfish is flanked by two fine rock-gardens reconstructed in 1968, one set with local coral rag, the other with 'Tufa' from Clwyd (Denbigh), both alkaline rocks.

To the west is the charming path and entrance to the Superintendent's house incorporating Jacob Bobart's 17th-century dwelling. Just in front of the house-fence stands a *Koelreuteria paniculata* or 'Pride of India', also known on account of its hanging fruits as the 'Golden Rain Tree', and next to it a *Paulownia tomentosa*, with great green sappy leaves, whose flowers give it the name of 'Foxglove Tree'. The area to the south is planted mainly with a great variety of apples, including crabs, and also with *Paliurus spina-Christi* (20 paces from the *Paulownia*), which rivals the holly's claim to have been the tree from which Christ's crown of thorns was made.

At the far end, in a straight line from the Danby Gate, is the Bog Garden, replacing the copper cisterns in which John Sibthorp had to keep his bog plants in the late 18th century. Liable to be flooded in winter, it grows thick with lush vegetation, unusual buttercups with little button heads (*Ranunculus acris* 'Flore pleno'), deep scarlet *Lobelia cardinalis*, the thick, tough leaves of *Rodgersia pinnata*,

51 Alstroemeria, *the Peruvian lily, provides a spectacular range of colours in the Bog Garden at the far end of the Botanic Garden.*

turning rusty gold in autumn, and *Peltaphyllum peltatum*, which puts up sprouts like hairy pink worms, later bearing white flowers on their heads, before developing giant thick-veined leaves. Later in the year luxuriant *Senecio tanguticus* with golden pyramids of flowers overtops everything. This is an ideal spot for a warm day, on a seat looking towards Christ Church Meadow. *Staphylea*, the bladdernut just at the rear of the Bog Garden, of which there are two species, has light green fruits looking as though they had been puffed full of air.

To return to the Danby Gate turn left and continue alongside a large area of shrubs: plenty of the well-known viburnums, *Philadelphus*, *Ribes*, *Diervilla*, *Deutzia*, lilac, spotted laurel, *Forsythia* and *Buddleia*, but also (where the path divides) the less familiar *Caragana boisii*, a form of Pea Tree. Also near here are *Corylopsis pauciflora* or winter hazel, and the delightful *Kolkwitzia amabilis*, known in America as the Beauty Bush (a profusion of pink trumpets in May and June). Between the walk and the Cherwell are many varieties of geranium species, also some of the plants and flowers in which the Garden specialises: roses, berberises, crocuses and euphorbias. Near the end where the path divides is a gigantic *Salix babylonica*, planted as recently as 1920, confronting an equally gigantic black walnut, near which is the much smaller and very much rarer *Phellodendron chinense*, planted in the same year, thirteen years after its introduction to this country.

This area, of great beauty during the flowering season, now gives way to the great array of roses extending as far as the rock-garden. The roses are arranged to show the main ancestral species and their varieties, the main hybrid varieties of the 19th and then the 20th century, hybrid varieties away from the main breeding lines, main varieties crossed with minor species, and minor species and their varieties. Help in understanding is provided by the Guide, with sketches and

52 Haemanthus Katherinae, *a native of Natal.*

53 *The effect of a jungle is created by silhouettes in the Botanic Garden hothouse.*

diagrams to show how the China roses combined with the European ones. All create a superb view of brilliant white and red roses rising up to meet Magdalen's ravishing tower on the skyline.

A fine herbaceous border stretches all along the south face of the fourteen-foot wall. Early in the year banks of purple and yellow irises set off the golden ivy on the pillar, and all through the year the border moves in colour from delphiniums and hollyhocks to sunflowers and Michaelmas daisies. In May, the low gateway over to the right has a spray of *Rosa* x *amadis* over the arch; with Canterbury bells in the foreground and 'horsetails' (*Equisetum*) in the background this makes everyone's picture of rural England.

Go through the gate, passing on the left a grotesque weeping ash and keeping alongside the eastern wall till you come to the stone arch leading to the greenhouses alongside the river. These are open only from 2 till 4 p.m. daily, and since the displays of smaller plants often change it is quite hard to see everything. In the Palm House, to your right as you come through the stone arch, coconut-oil and date palms, tea, coffee and cacao are an attraction that children particularly like. So is the Telegraph Plant, *Desmodium gyrans*, with stipules at the base which rotate continually, as though signalling. Equally curious is the Sensitive Plant, *Mimosa pudica*, a specimen of which was shown here to John Evelyn in July 1654. Its leaves close in on themselves at the slightest touch. A special collection is kept of insect-eating plants, Venus's fly-trap, *Sarracenia flava* and other pitcher plants resembling tall conical jugs, which, with their gaping red mouths, attract insects to enter their slippery slopes and skid over the downward pointing hairs that prevent escape. These are in the Succulent House at the far end of the right-hand

greenhouses, where there are also two clumps of *Strelitzia reginae*, their orange and purple pointed flowers like inquisitive birds' heads thrusting out from reeds in all directions. Also here are cacti and *Agaves* from the deserts of North and South America, euphorbias and aloes from Africa. One of the most ancient plants still in existence is *Cycas revoluta*, with long leaves armed on both sides like the weaponed jaw of a swordfish. Another is *Encephelartos*, whose fruit is worth watching from week to week, after the end of May, as it develops from inside unfolding inter-clasping leaves and finally grows into a two-foot-long banana-shaped pine-cone or pineapple. Much of the Earth was covered with vegetation like this in Mesozoic times.

Also in the Succulent House is a cone of blue and pink flowers that seem to be decorating a Christmas tree several feet above ground – the top grows a good seven feet high. This is *Echium wildprettii*, a kind of borage from the Canary Islands. The cactuses themselves, for which the House was built, are nearing the roof.

Coming back through the narrow Temperate Corridor, you brush past tree fuchsias, *Abutilons*, and in spring arum lilies and *Clivias*. Crossing then through the open air to the other greenhouses, you will probably have to forego the orchids in the first room, which is shut because they are too tempting to collectors. But carry on along the Tropical Corridor under *Passiflora quadrangularis* and a yam, to the next room, famous for its lily pool. This was originally built for the huge Amazon water-lily, with leaves big enough to support a weight of many pounds. Now it has twenty species and varieties of *Nymphaea* in at least four colours, while beds have the Sacred Lotus, the sugar cane, and the banana. Further down the corridor are ferns, and last of all an Alpine House, which holds not only alpines but dwarf trees:

54 *One of several flowering cherries which stand by the Cherwell as it flows past the Botanic Garden.*

Sequoia sempervirens 'Prostrata' makes a great contrast with the more familiar *Sequoiadendron giganteum* or wellingtonias. It is possible to walk straight out of the Alpine House on to the banks of the Cherwell, with the collection of willows on the farther bank, though the cherries (**54**) on the nearer side bid for all your attention in spring. They are among the most beautiful of all Japanese cherries: the early pink *Prunus* 'Shimidsu Sakura', *P.* 'Kiku-shidare Sakura', the columnar *P.* 'Amanogawa', and the very young *P. serrulata* 'Asano', the last three with brilliant white blossoms (also a *P. serrula* notable for its bark). Almost equally white throughout the winter is the bark of *Betula jacquemontii*, well-placed beside the darkened yellow arches of the 18th-century road-bridge.

Here the path turns left and re-enters the main, enclosed garden, protective and peaceful, not as it used to be in Victorian times, when it was more like a public park, but crammed with interest. Demonstration beds occupy the first rows nearest the entrance to each section. Apart from irises arranged in increasing order of chromosome number there are also beds demonstrating variegation in plants, hybrids and chimaeras, all partly explained on the plaques.

These were special interests of a past Director and Superintendent, instances of three hundred years of experiment and research in the oldest Botanic Garden still surviving in Britain. It was here that in the 1660s Jacob Bobart the Younger came across a seedling in which the occidental and oriental plane had crossed, producing the London plane now planted in every big city in the country. (The case on behalf of John Tradescant as the discoverer is too slight.) Oxford can also claim to have contributed in the late 17th century to the proof of sexuality in plants. The

55 *The fantastically shaped* Lilium speciosum, *a native of Japan, gives off a delicate fragrance like vanilla.*

collections made by Professor Sherard, after whom the Chair of Botany is named, while consul at Smyrna, still form part of the present herbarium. Two Oxford botanists were honoured by the great Swedish botanist Linnaeus: *Sibthorpia europea* is named after Humphrey Sibthorp, *Dillenia* after James Dillen. A greater Oxford achievement is celebrated just outside the Garden, where the rose garden commemorates the work done in the University on penicillin.

The Genetic Garden

The Botanic Garden shows the fact of evolution. The Genetic Garden, about half a mile away and overlooking University Parks, illustrates evolutionary mechanisms, such as gene and chromosome mutation and hybridisation, without which there could be no evolutionary change. Though open only to members of the University when a gardener is present, unless by special arrangement, this is not too specialised for a layman to enjoy, and a visit in May, passing the eleven flowering cherries outside the Physical Chemistry Building off South Parks Road, gives added pleasure. The winding grass paths and wooden seats invite contemplation as well as study, and there are enough strange plants to cause some wonder: antirrhinum 'Bizarre' is aptly named, and the corkscrew branches of some willows are a curiosity. Cabbages grow here with leaves changing from yellow to mauve, purple and green within the one plant. The medieval *Rosa mundi* illustrates the 'colour break' caused by instability resulting in a change in a cell. Tomatoes red and gamboge are shaped like plums and pears and cucumbers, ivies put out flowering shoots rather than new ordinary climbing ones. With 'sports' of these

56 *The Arboretum of the University at Nuneham Courtenay, outside the city, has many fine rhodendrons, including this R. 'Elizabeth', first raised at Bodnant in Wales.*

kinds Nature as well as Man tries out forms and colours and keeps what works. 'Monster', 'Chimaeras', 'Mosaic Infection' and much besides is explained (up to a point) in the official Guide. A longer, ten-page typescript is usually available from a small covered tray inside the Garden itself.

Nuneham Courtenay

The University Arboretum (**57**), a few miles out of town off the Maidenhead road, has been open to the public since 1969, and can now be visited from April to September. It is a magnificent collection of North American conifers, some of which are recorded as among the first of their species to be planted in Great Britain. An incense cedar had already reached 59 feet in height and 7 feet in girth by 1908, while a white spruce (*Picea glauca*), one of the most important timber trees of Canada, had reached 67 feet by 1932. Silver firs, monkey-puzzle trees, Oregon Douglas firs and wellingtonias are among the many other species, though many trees were lost in the gales of March 1986. There are also plantations of willows, near the pond, Scots pines on Windmill Hill, Lucombe oaks near the southernmost point of the Arboretum, and oaks near the Peacock Gate. Peacocks abound, and will open their fans at every opportunity.

As there is an outcrop of Lower Greensand here, there are massed rhododendrons (**56**), azaleas, magnolias, camellias and heathers, seldom seen in Oxfordshire, in addition to certain rare Chilean shrubs. There is also a bluebell wood and an avenue of maples.

Index

A selection of plants, shrubs and trees mentioned in the text, not including those in the Botanic Garden.

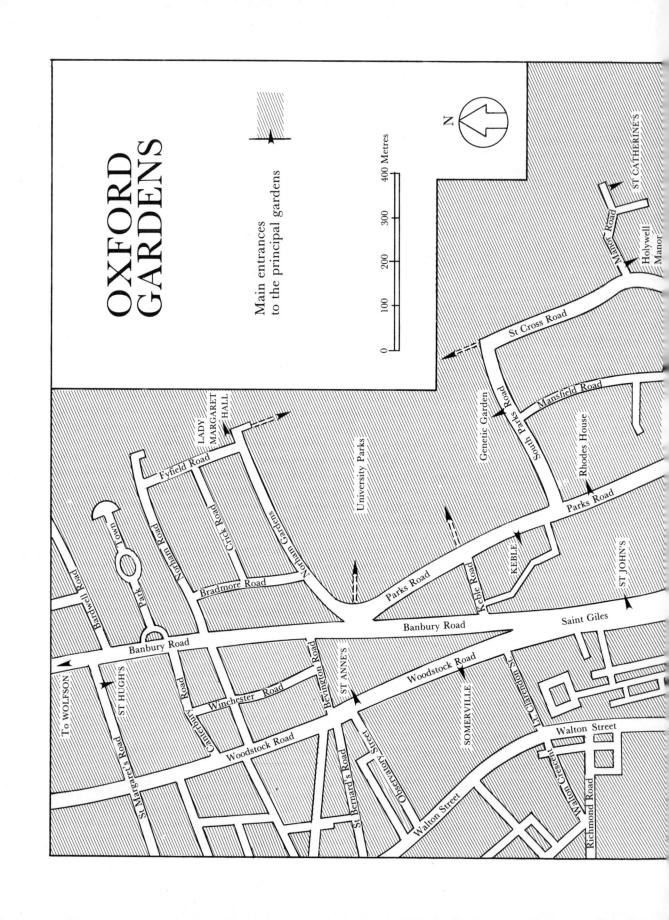

OXFORD GARDENS

Main entrances
to the principal gardens

0   100   200   300   400 Metres

N